World Geography

TIME LIFE Student Library

World Geography

Time-Life Books   Alexandria, Virginia

Table of **Contents**

What Is Geography?

Where are the world's highest mountains? How many babies are born in Moose Jaw, Saskatchewan? Which animals live in Africa? You can answer these questions when you study **geography.**

The word "geography" comes from Greek words that mean to write about or study the earth. **Geographers** want to know why one place is different from another. That means they study the **physical** land: its shape, its animals, and its **climate.** They also study people and how they fit into their **environment.** Geographers learn where people build towns, how they use **natural resources,** and how they set up their government, transportation, and communication. Piece by piece, geographers combine these bits of information to build a complete picture of a region. Geography helps us understand how people and places are connected —and how they are unique.

The students below know that geography is about people like them, explaining both their differences and their common bonds. It is also about the physical world, such as this wall of ice in Tibet *(right),* scaled by a lone climber.

Earth's Surface Water

W e live on a blue planet. More than two-thirds of the earth is covered by a vast expanse of salt water sometimes called the World **Ocean.** Although we call different segments the Atlantic, Pacific, Indian, and Arctic Oceans, they are parts of a connected body of water. Yet the Pacific alone is so large that all of the land on earth could fit inside it—with room to spare.

Like a global thermostat, oceans regulate world **climate** by storing, redistributing, and releasing heat. They also provide most of the water that plants, animals, and humans need. In a process called the **water cycle,** water evaporates from the surface of the oceans, lakes, and **rivers,** adding water vapor to the air. The vapor travels through the atmosphere and condenses as it cools, falling back into the oceans or on land as rain and snow. Then the cycle begins again.

Pacific Ocean

Oceans in Motion

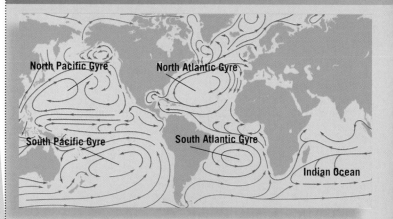

North Pacific Gyre

North Atlantic Gyre

South Pacific Gyre

South Atlantic Gyre

Indian Ocean

Current Affair

Currents move through oceans in sweeping circular patterns called **gyres.** They help to keep the global climate stable by moving warm water (*red arrows*) to cool regions (*blue arrows*) and bringing cooler water back to warm regions. Deep in the ocean, currents slowly circulate oxygen and other nutrients.

Where on EARTH?

Strange Seascape

C rusty formations poke through the salty surface of the Dead Sea, which lies on the border between Israel and Jordan. At 408 m (1,339 ft.) below sea level, the shore of the Dead Sea is the lowest exposed point on earth. Though it is actually an inland lake, the Dead Sea's mineral-rich waters are eight times as salty as any ocean. When the water evaporates, it leaves behind bizarre shapes (*left*). The high salt concentration makes life nearly impossible here, which is how this barren "sea" earned its forbidding name.

Secrets of the Deep

Far from the curling waves that carry this windsurfer, oceans drop to an average depth of 4 km (2.5 mi.). In this dark world lie earth's deepest canyons, its longest **mountain** range, and more than 80 percent of all life on earth. Scientists estimate that as much as 98 percent of the ocean remains to be explored.

Frozen Ocean

Polar bears can travel for miles as they hunt for a snack on the Arctic ice. Unlike the Antarctic, which is land, the Arctic is an ocean. Most of it is covered by giant islands of ice, called pack ice, that can be 9.6 km (6 mi.) long and 200 m (656 ft.) thick. Summertime brings an abundance of whales, seals, and many kinds of fish to feed in the slightly warmer water.

Erosion

Since 1893, storms and pounding waves have narrowed the strip of land between the lighthouse and the sea at Cape Hatteras in North Carolina from 1,600 m (5,280 ft.) to 36 m (120 ft.). Waves and wind are constantly eroding and reshaping the coast.

1993

1893

A Drop in the Bucket

About 97 percent of earth's water is contained in its deep oceans. Most of the remainder is permanently frozen in icecaps and glaciers or stored as **ground water.** In all, less than 1 percent of earth's water flows in its many rivers, lakes, and streams.

At Sutherland Falls in New Zealand *(right)*, meltwater from snow collects in Lake Quill, then spills 579 m (1,900 ft.) to the Arthur River below. Lakes act like big bowls, collecting water dumped by rivers or running off the mountains. In contrast, rivers are constantly in motion. As they flow to their end in lakes or the sea they reshape the land, sometimes carving deep valleys such as the Grand Canyon.

Earth's Surface Land

As you read this page, the land below you is moving. Earth's crust (its thin, rocky outer layer) is broken into about a dozen pieces, called plates. These plates float like rafts on the hot, partly liquid interior of the earth. They are slowly colliding and pulling apart.

As they grind along, the plates push up **mountains,** cause earthquakes to rumble, and trigger volcanic eruptions. These large-scale movements of the crust shape the **continents** from the inside.

As soon as mountains are pushed up by **plate tectonics,** wind, water, and ice begin to wear them away. These forces on the earth's surface shape the land from the outside. Over millions of years, even the tallest mountains will be worn down by weathering and **erosion.**

Lay of the Land

Mountains, valleys, **plains,** and **plateaus** are names we give to common features of the land. Some terms are specialized: An escarpment, for instance, is a cliff that separates two flat pieces of land at different levels. Often, the larger features influence the **climate** of a region and the way life must adapt there. Rain clouds often get trapped on one side of a mountain range, so that one side may be lush and green, and the other, which is said to lie in a rain shadow, is **desert.** The illustration at left shows many common land features collected in one imaginary landscape.

Volcano
Mountain Peak
Mountains
Desert
Sand Dunes
Mesa
Dome Rock
Butte
Canyon
U-Shaped Valley
Lake
Escarpment
Cuff
Snowfield
Tributary Plain
River
Bay
River Delta
Peninsula
Glacier
Ocean
Island
Iceberg

Ice Riders

Like a giant bulldozer, the Black Rapids Glacier carved this valley in Alaska, where bicyclists now ride. Glaciers are giant sheets of compacted snow and ice up to 100 m (330 ft.) thick that often form high in the mountains and creep downhill, pulled by their immense weight. Glaciers carve deep, U-shaped valleys and pick up rocks, boulders, and other **debris** as they go. About 10 percent of the earth's land is permanently covered by glacial ice.

Getting Physical

Mapmakers usually divide the earth's largest landmasses into seven continents. Some, such as Australia and Antarctica, are really huge islands. The continents of Europe and Asia belong to one piece of land but represent very different **cultures** and **environments**.

Would **You** *Believe?*

Piecing It Together

Riding on earth's moving plates, today's continents have traveled a lot in 200 million years. At one time they fit together like pieces in a giant jigsaw puzzle; South America was once tucked into West Africa. Scientists predict that in another hundred million years, Africa will squeeze closer to Europe, whereas North and South America will separate completely.

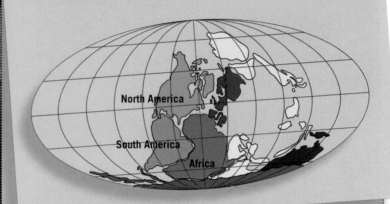

Whose Fault Is This?

Steam rises from a gaping crack in Iceland *(below)*. The North Atlantic island of Iceland lies along the Mid-Atlantic Ridge, a long line of underwater mountains that marks where two plates are separating under the ocean. As the plates move apart, the earth above them is being torn open. Molten magma bubbles up through the crack, forming new land as it cools. Because of this spreading under the Atlantic, North America and Europe are moving away from each other at a rate of about 2.5 cm (1 in.) per year.

Mapping Our World

Making Maps Today

Every map displays a mapmaker's ideas about the world. Ancient maps included imaginary places and the legendary beasts who were thought to live there. Early European mapmakers drew maps that showed their religious ideas of humans' place in the universe, rather than lands in relation to other lands. After about the year 1400, however, **geographers** began to make more accurate maps. Explorers sailed down the coasts of Africa and Asia and across the Atlantic with improved surveying instruments, bringing back the latest information about distances and **terrain.** Today's geographers use the science of remote sensing by aerial photography, radar, and satellite imagery to help them capture an up-to-the-minute portrait of our changeable earth's features. With the help of computers, they put that information together to make maps of everything from ozone depletion to deforestation in Brazil.

Columbia 1983

Mount Everest
(8,848 m   29,028 ft.)

Austrian Survey
1955

Constant Change

Maps need regular updating. Not only do people change country borders and names, but the earth itself changes. In November 1963, for example, an **island** suddenly appeared in the Atlantic Ocean off the coast of Iceland. Volcanic eruptions under the sea built up 2.6 sq km (1 sq mi.) of new land, which rose to a mound 170 m (558 ft.) high. The island was named Surtsey, after an ancient god of fire.

Would You Believe?

Photography, satellites, and computers have caused the art of **cartography** to be transformed. Satellites in space record many kinds of information: sunlight reflected from the ground, radar waves that show the height of **mountains,** even the heat that is given off by cities, vegetation, and water. The satellites send this information to computers on the ground in a number code. Mapmakers then work with the computers *(above, right),* using a kind of software called a GIS, or geographic information system, to make a variety of maps. Not everything is done with this kind of remote sensing, however. On the ground, people make measurements at sample spots to verify results from aerial surveys. They also collect place names, population figures, and other cultural features that will be shown on the maps.

Charting the Oceans

A Mountainous Ocean Floor

A cartographer puts the finishing touches on a relief map of the ocean floor near Antarctica. Maps of the water are as important as maps of the land. Sailors and scientists alike need to know shorelines, depths of water, islands, obstructions, tides, and currents. Satellites, survey ships, and aerial photos all supply the information.

Time Zones

Because we tell time by the sun, our position on earth determines what time it is. To keep the whole world on one system, people divided the earth into time zones in 1884. By international agreement, they established exact areas within which time would be considered the same. They also set a beginning and ending place for each day at the International Date Line, a **longitude** line in the Pacific Ocean. Time advances one hour for every zone you pass through going around the globe from west to east.

Map Projections

To show a round earth on a flat piece of paper, mapmakers divide the earth's surface into regular segments with a grid of lines crossing at right angles. Then they "project" the grid onto a flat surface, so that landmasses on a map will have the same relation to each other as on a globe, although their sizes or shapes are distorted. In the diagram at left, called a **Mercator projection,** flattening the grid has changed the relative sizes of South America and Greenland. On the globe, as on the earth, South America is really much larger than Greenland.

Latitude

The **equator** is an imaginary line circling the earth between the North and South Poles. Lines of **latitude** are drawn parallel to it and increase from 0° to 90°. They are called degrees of north and south latitude, depending on whether they are north or south of the equator.

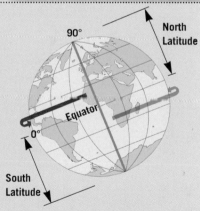

Longitude

Geographers divide the globe into 360 imaginary lines radiating from the poles that go from a 0° line passing through Greenwich, England, east and west to a 180° line passing through the Fiji Islands. Lines west of Greenwich are "degrees of west longitude," to the east, "east longitude."

Reading Maps

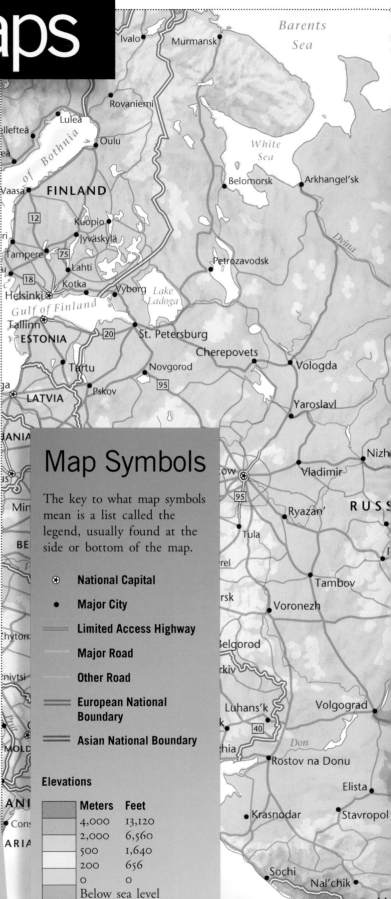

Every map leads to treasure—to a wealth of information about the **climate,** landscape, people, and history of the place that it portrays. Learn a map's symbols, and you will uncover its secrets. Want to know which way is up? Most maps have directional arrows or a **compass rose** that shows north (N) at the top, south (S) at the bottom, east (E) at the right, and west (W) at the left. Then check the map's key, or legend. It tells you what features the map includes, and how they are shown. For example, a capital city may be a circle with a star; a major city is shown as a dot. The **scale** gives you a ruler that shows how distance on the map compares with distance in the real world. Special symbols show **mountains,** airports, and political borders. Other symbols use colors and shading to tell you if the land has trees or sand, lakes or swamps. Finally, lines and degrees of **latitude** and **longitude** will pinpoint your location anywhere on earth.

Finding Your Way

The curious tourists at left are using a street map to find the sights in London, England. Most maps are divided into squares (grids). Letters along one edge of the map and numbers at right angles to them identify each square. The map index shows a letter and number combination, like G-5, for each place or street on the map. Sight along the G line till it intersects the 5 line to find the place or street you are looking for.

Map Symbols

The key to what map symbols mean is a list called the legend, usually found at the side or bottom of the map.

- ⊗ **National Capital**
- • **Major City**
- ═ **Limited Access Highway**
- ─ **Major Road**
- ─ **Other Road**
- ═ **European National Boundary**
- ═ **Asian National Boundary**

Elevations

	Meters	Feet
	4,000	13,120
	2,000	6,560
	500	1,640
	200	656
	0	0
	Below sea level	

```
0        50        100 mi.
0     50    100 km
```

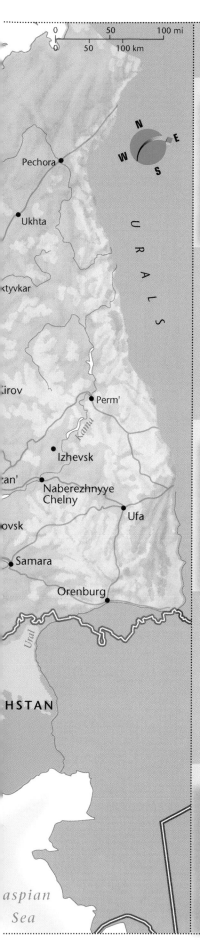

Kinds of Maps

Physical Maps

Physical maps reflect the land-scape of an area, showing rivers, lakes, **deserts,** mountains, and other natural features. Some may also show human additions, such as cities or country borders.

Political Maps

Political maps show boundaries between countries. Borders may run along rivers or mountains or be straight lines. These maps can change quickly after wars, when land may be redistributed, or through alliances.

Road Maps

Road maps show—guess what?—roads! Major high-ways and smaller roads may appear in different colors. Some road maps mark the distances between places.

Street Maps

Really a specialized road map, the street map shows a close-up view of streets in a limited area. You can follow this map to walk from one address to another in town and even find buildings or parks.

Pilot Charts

Airplane pilots use aeronautical maps. These specialized charts show heights of obstacles like mountains, the locations of features like lakes and **rivers,** major flight paths, and air-ports large and small.

Would You Believe?

Navigation Aids

The pile of stones above is an *inukshuk* built long ago at Hudson Strait by Inuit travelers. Such piles were signposts in the Arctic landscape where there are few natural land-marks to help in navigation. A different kind of old map made of bamboo strips *(below)* shows currents, prevailing winds, and the position of **islands**—symbolized by the small shells—to people sailing across wide distances of the Pacific Ocean in canoes.

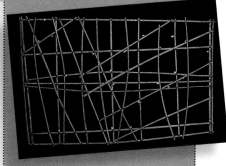

Environments and Biomes

Although no two landscapes look exactly alike, scientists are able to group them into about 10 zones, called **biomes,** based on similarities in plant and animal life. **Geography** and **climate** determine what kind of biome a region will have. **Deserts** form, for example, where little rain falls. **Forests** need a lot of rain and warm growing days to survive.

Similar biomes can usually be found in similar **latitudes,** moving north and south from the **equator.** Near the equator, where the sun's rays are strongest, lie rain forests, hot deserts, and tropical **grasslands** called **savannas.** Farther north and south the climate becomes **temperate,** and regions experience distinct seasons. Here are the grasslands and **deciduous** forests. Even farther from the equator lie **coniferous** forests, which give way to **tundra.** Finally, at the northern and southern ends of the earth are the polar regions, buried beneath permanent layers of ice and snow.

World Biomes

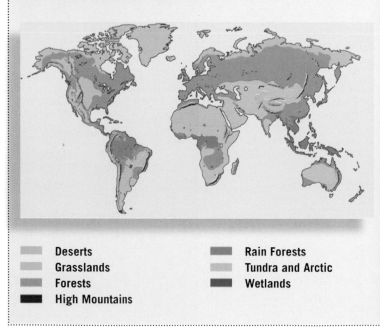

- Deserts
- Grasslands
- Forests
- High Mountains
- Rain Forests
- Tundra and Arctic
- Wetlands

One Country, Lots of Biomes

The spectacular Andes Mountains *(below)*, which run through the middle of Peru, are only one of the country's many **habitat** zones. **Rain forest** covers more than half of the eastern part of Peru, and a strip of desert runs along its cool coast. Between the peaks of the Andes stretch high fertile **plateaus,** called the **altiplano,** where Peruvians grow potatoes and corn. On higher plateaus llamas and alpacas graze the cool grasslands.

Earth under Glass

In this strange-looking building lie a tropical rain forest, desert, farm, and mini-**ocean.** Scientists built the Biosphere II project *(below)* in the Arizona desert to see if they could re-create earth's complex **ecosystem.** Researchers survived locked inside for two years without any outside help, but dangerous levels of carbon dioxide began to build up, and they had to stop the experiment. The project gave scientists insights into the delicate balance of life on earth, proving it a difficult design to copy. Today, Biosphere II is a research center where scientists test the effects of environmental changes on the earth.

Adapting to the Habitat

Many animals develop special traits to ensure survival in their habitats. Baby harp seals *(above)* are born white, to hide them from predators in the snowy Arctic. As they grow older and move faster, they turn gray. The addax *(right)*, an antelope that lives in the dry scrublands of Africa, can survive without water. It gets its liquids from leaves.

Grasslands

rasses blanket more than one-third of the land on earth. They stretch over wide, flat regions where rainfall is between 250 and 750 mm (10 and 30 in.) per year. That's a little too wet for a **desert** and too dry to support a **forest** of trees, but it's just right for grasses and cereals.

Grasses are hardy plants. They are able to survive frequent grazing by sprouting new growth from their base instead of their tip. The more they are nibbled on, the more they grow. Though they look wide and empty, **grasslands** are richly fertile lands, capable of supporting more large animals per acre than any other **habitat** on earth. Few animals can hide in grasslands. Large animals, such as giraffes or zebras, move in herds for protection from predators. Smaller animals, such as prairie dogs, dig burrows and hide underground.

Where in the World?

Grasslands

Home Sweet Yurt

Yurts, or gers *(above)*, are the traditional homes of **nomadic** horse and yak herders living on the vast, dry **steppes** of Mongolia and central Asia. Made of felt and stretched over a collapsible wooden frame, the tents are sturdy and warm but also easy to pack up and move with the herds to greener pastures.

Gauchos on the Pampas

Argentine gauchos *(below)* drive a herd of cattle across the **pampas,** the fertile grasslands of South America. Beef raised on large pampas ranches, called estancias, is highly prized and exported all over the world. Like the cowboys of North America's West, gauchos have a long, rich history of independence and toughness. In the past, they rode their horses barefoot, gripping the stirrups between their toes.

Would **You** *Believe?*

Biker Dogs

Motorcycles are a quick way for shepherds to get around on Australia's flat grasslands, where the sheep outnumber people 10 to 1. Sheepdogs are essential for keeping the large herds in line, and sometimes these hardworking animals hitch a ride.

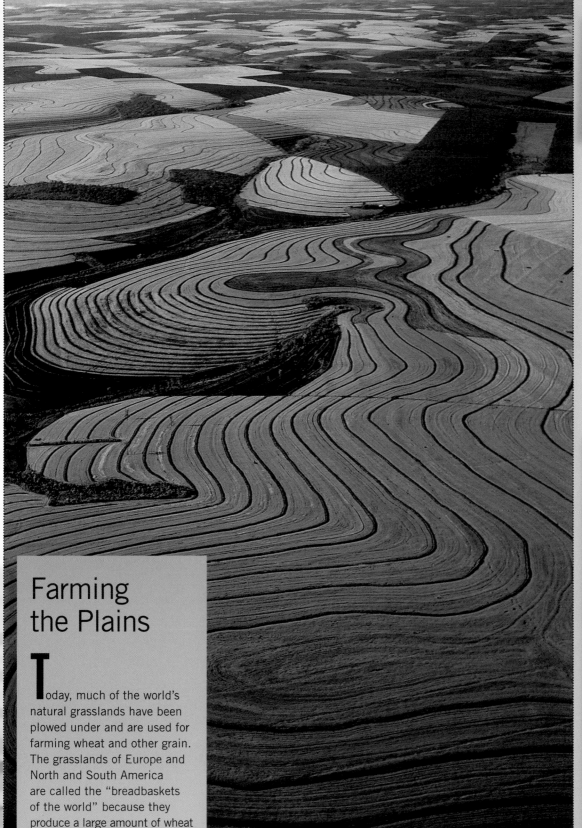

African Savanna

Giraffes, zebras, and lions roam the tropical grassland, or **savanna,** in Africa's Serengeti National Park. Sparsely covered with drought-resistant grasses and acacia trees, savannas are found near the **equator.** They have only a brief rainy season.

Dust Bowl

Overuse of grassland for farming, combined with a major drought during the 1930s, caused the Dust Bowl, one of the worst farming disasters in U.S. history. Millions of acres of crops withered and died, while precious topsoil turned to dust and blew across the flat land of the Midwest, burying entire farms, like the one above, and turning the land into unproductive wasteland.

Farming the Plains

Today, much of the world's natural grasslands have been plowed under and are used for farming wheat and other grain. The grasslands of Europe and North and South America are called the "breadbaskets of the world" because they produce a large amount of wheat and corn. This field in Brazil has been plowed into contours and planted with varied crops to prevent soil **erosion.**

Deserts The Dry Land

Deserts are vast, dry regions that cover about one-fifth of the land surface of the earth. They can be freezing cold like Antarctica, or scorchingly hot, like the Sahara. Desert **terrain** can be rocky, mountainous, or covered by shifting sands. About the only thing the world's **deserts** have in common is their dryness: They receive an average of less than 250 mm (10 in.) of rain per year. In some years, they receive no rain at all.

Life in the desert is hard. Plants and animals have had to adapt to scarce amounts of food and water. Many desert animals are **nocturnal,** hunting only during the cool of night to conserve energy. Desert plants can store water for many months while they wait out long seasons of drought. Despite these hardships, a surprising variety of wildlife, and people, call the desert home.

Where in the World?

Deserts

Roaming Rocks

Would You Believe?

Rocks like these, which weigh up to 45 kg (100 lb.), are making tracks across Death Valley in California. Scientists believe that a small bit of moisture in the clay of the desert soil makes it slippery enough for a gust of wind to send these flat-bottomed rocks sliding across the desert floor.

One Lump or Two?

Double-humped Bactrian camels, found only in Asia, cross the Gobi Desert in western China. The Gobi, which means "waterless place" in Mongolian, stretches for an area six times larger than the United Kingdom across Asia. Rain-filled clouds from the Atlantic and Pacific Oceans spill their waters long before they reach the area, leaving the land parched and dry.

Busy Blooms

After an early spring rainfall, the Sonoran Desert in Arizona *(below)* explodes with colorful wildflowers. Sometimes called quick-response plants, these desert plants must take advantage of seasonal rain by flowering and reproducing quickly, before the oppressive heat of summer dries out the land again. Some plants lie dormant through many years of drought, waiting for the right amount of rain to fall before they rush into bloom again.

Oasis—a Refuge of Green

This oasis in the Sahara is a fertile island of green in an otherwise barren landscape. A rare, steady supply of water supports plant life, such as the date palms above.

To reach an oasis, water must travel long distances below the surface through an **aquifer,** an underground system of porous rock. Where the aquifer is cracked or the land above it has been worn away by **erosion,** water bubbles to the surface, and an oasis forms. The very survival of the people and animals of the desert depends on the year-round water supply at an oasis.

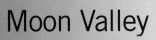

Where on EARTH?

Moon Valley

The desolate landscape at right isn't on the moon, but it looks like it. The Valley of the Moon is part of the Atacama Desert, which runs along the coast of Chile for 3,217 km (2,000 mi.). It is the driest spot on earth, receiving less than 0.08 mm (0.003 in.) of rain per year. The cause is the cold Humboldt Current in the Pacific Ocean. Air masses along this coast are chilled and hold little water vapor, so rain seldom falls on the parched land.

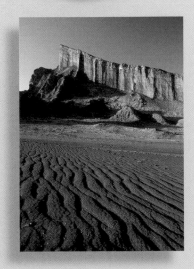

Desert People

More than one billion people live in the deserts of the world, including these young Bedouins from Jordan. Bedouin are **nomadic** people who herd camels and transport goods by caravan through the deserts of the Middle East. The boys' headpieces and long robes protect them from blowing sand and insulate them against the unforgiving desert sun while allowing air to circulate underneath. Bedouins cross borders freely, caring little about which country they are in.

Forests Temperate and Cool

Forests cover about 20 percent of the land surface of the earth. Inside a **forest** it is moist and cool. The leafy canopy above blocks most of the sun's rays. This dense vegetation, which requires more than 750 mm (30 in.) of rain per year, also blocks most of the wind, making forests a stable **environment** for plants and animals to grow.

The kinds of trees that thrive in a forest are determined by climate and geography. **Coniferous** forests grow in colder, northern climates or on high **mountains.** Conifers have thin, needlelike leaves and stay green year round. Farther south, where the seasons change, **deciduous** forests flourish. Deciduous trees have large, broad leaves that change colors and fall to the ground in autumn. This helps them conserve water through the long, dry winters.

Where in the World?

Forests

This Will Make You Smaller

Like the storybook mushroom that made Alice shrink in *Alice in Wonderland*, real mushrooms help to make dead trees smaller. When trees die and fall on the forest floor, mushrooms sprout on the rotting wood and use its nutrients to grow. The mushrooms speed a tree's decomposition by breaking down its **organic** material and returning chemicals from the wood to the soil and atmosphere. These chemicals will in turn support the growth of a new tree.

Deciduous

As deciduous trees, such as oak, hickory, or maple, respond to the shorter days of the coming winter and lack of available water, they stop making chlorophyll, and their leaves lose the green of summer. The shades of their brilliant autumn hues are determined by yellow and orange pigments that remain in the leaves and also by levels of sugar, which produce red and violet hues.

Coniferous

Coniferous trees have waxy, needlelike leaves that lose little water. This allows them to stay "evergreen." Conifers get their name from the hard, woody cones they produce. The cones protect the seeds inside. These seeds are spread by the wind when they have ripened.

Acid Rain

The researchers at right are collecting fish samples from a Massachusetts stream to test for the effects of **acid rain.** Acid rain falls when pollutants released by factories and power plants travel through the atmosphere, mixing with clouds and falling to earth in raindrops. Often clouds full of pollutants drift from industrial areas poisoning the land and water in areas that produce little local pollution. Acid rain destroys nutrients in the soil and cripples fresh-water **ecosystems.** Lack of nutrients makes trees weak and no longer resistant to disease *(far right).*

Rising acidity in lakes and streams has threatened many species of fish and plants to near extinction. Forests in North America and Europe are in serious danger of destruction unless something is done to stop the pollution in the air.

How Tall?

110 m (360 ft.)   98 m (320 ft.)   74 m (243 ft.)

Redwoods

What is 2,000 years old and taller than both America's Statue of Liberty and India's Taj Mahal? A California redwood. Redwoods are the tallest trees on the planet. Named for the color of their bark and wood, redwoods are remarkably hardy trees. Their bark has a high amount of a natural acid called tannin, which prevents insects and disease from doing any damage to the wood. This strong bark also protects red-woods from periodic forest fires.

Bamboo Forests

A rare panda stops to snack in China's bamboo forest. Bamboo, which is actually a treelike grass, grows tall in lush forests in southwest Asia. Pandas eat about 40 percent of their body weight in bamboo per day. With advancing development in China, bamboo forests are cut down for farmland and timber, and the pandas are losing their **habitat.**

Rain Forests Dark Jungles

Rain Forest Layers

1. Emergent Layer Emergents, the tallest trees, break through the dense rain forest canopy, rising to 60 m (200 ft.).

2. Canopy This thick tangle of treetops absorbs 98 percent of the sun's rays and is home to most of the rain forest's animals.

3. Understory The shady understory is protected from wind and storms. Here shrubs, young trees, and climbing vines grow.

4. Forest Floor Fewer things grow on the forest floor, which receives only about 2 percent of the light from above.

Rain forests are found near the **equator,** where the **climate** is wet and warm. These **forests** get an average of 2,000 mm (80 in.) of rain per year, and some years up to five times as much. The combination of intense sunlight and plentiful rain has produced a diverse range of plants and animals. Though **rain forests** cover only 6 percent of the earth's land surface, they are home to more than half of the plant and animal species. Scientists predict that there are millions more yet to be discovered.

Like a global air conditioner, rain forests keep the earth cool by absorbing the sun's heat in their dark, leafy canopies. They take in carbon dioxide from the atmosphere and release oxygen through **photosynthesis.** When rain forests are cut down, this delicate process is destroyed, and the earth heats up.

Where in the World?

Rain Forests

Colorful Creatures

The darkness of the rain forest is colored by many bright species. The rainbow-striped toucan *(left)* has a beak as long as its body. The bright color of the poison-arrow frog *(below, left)* is a warning to predators to stay away. Rain forest people rub arrows on the frog's skin, which is poisonous, to make deadly hunting weapons.

Forest on Fire

Once, slash-and-burn clearing *(right)* was an acceptable way for farmers to gain forest land for cultivation. After a few years, they moved on, and let the jungle reclaim the land. Now more and more people are clearing land this way. But large-scale farming depletes the soil. The land becomes useless as farmland in a few years, and rain forests can no longer grow there either.

The raft at left was dropped by the giant blimp above. It is a portable research station, to help scientists explore the dense rain forest canopy teeming with animal species. Because it is difficult to climb from tree to tree, netting between the spokes of the wheel-shaped raft lets researchers move without having to come down.

Rain Forest Riches

Would You Believe?

Cacao Beans

These cacao beans from Brazil are ground up to be turned into chocolate. Translated, the name of the cacao tree means "food of the gods."

Rubber Tree

A woman in Southeast Asia taps latex from a rubber tree, which can produce up to 7 kg (15 lb.) a year. The sticky liquid is processed into rubber.

Diesel Tree

The copaiba tree from the Brazilian rain forest produces a sap that can run a diesel engine. Copaiba oil is difficult to harvest in large quantities, but in Brazil, about 20 percent of all gasoline comes from other plants, primarily sugarcane to make ethanol. Unlike oil drilled from the earth, plants are a renewable resource.

Tundra & Arctic

Polar **climates** are found in the extreme north and south of the earth near the poles. They are covered with permanently frozen snow and ice called icecaps. It is so cold at the poles that little rain or snow falls.

In the Northern Hemisphere, the land above 66½° of **latitude** is called the Arctic. This includes the frozen Arctic Ocean and the permanently ice-covered land that surrounds it, as well as **tundra,** which stretches between the end of the permanent ice and the beginning of the **tree line.** Only the top few inches of tundra thaw in the summer. The rest, called **permafrost,** remains frozen all year round.

North Pole

South Pole

Let's Compare

North Pole vs. South Pole

Permanent ice covers both poles, but at the North Pole *(below, left)*, the ice is the frozen Arctic Ocean. At the South Pole *(below, right)*, ice blankets the land of Antarctica. Both regions have months of total light and darkness, but at opposite times of the year.

What's a Pingo?

Like pimples popping from the frozen tundra, pingos are mounds of ice, forced to the surface as water trapped in the permafrost freezes and expands. Tundra vegetation of hardy grass and **lichens** grows over the top of the pingo, but the core remains frozen solid. This pingo in Greenland rises to 45 m (150 ft.) above the flat tundra landscape.

Beneath Arctic Ice

In spite of its freezing temperatures, there is much for divers to explore in the Arctic Ocean. The cold waters provide a perfect growing **environment** for plankton, which draws whales to the Arctic to feed. Other sea life includes brightly colored starfish, sea urchins, seals, and fish.

Arctic People

Inuit

Bouncing high on a walrus-skin blanket, this Inuit girl is participating in the Naluktaq, or Blanket Toss. The event is part of a larger festival held each year in northern Alaska to celebrate the end of a successful whaling season.

The Saami

With reindeer in tow, a Saami boy is making his way across the frozen tundra. His home is Lapland, part of northern Scandinavia and Russia's Kola Peninsula. The Saami in this icy land herd reindeer for their meat, hides, and milk, and use them as beasts of burden.

Where on EARTH?

Midnight Sun

During summer the sun never sets across Arctic landscapes. The earth is tilted on its axis toward the sun, which never has a chance to sink below the horizon. In winter, the earth is tilted the opposite way, and the land is dark for months.

High Mountains

Mountain **climates** are stacked like slices in a layer cake, becoming harsher and less hospitable closer to the peak. **Forests** or **grasslands** are usually found at a mountain's base. As the **altitude** increases, the climate becomes cooler, and a range of **biomes** occur. The **tree line** marks where trees will no longer grow because of cold temperatures and lack of rain. Beyond this point lie **alpine** meadows, which are characterized by low plants that withstand high winds and a short growing season. If a **mountain** is tall and wet enough, alpine meadows give way to gravel, rock, and a permanent cap of snow.

High in the mountains, the air is thinner, and oxygen is low. This air cannot hold heat or water very well. Thus, temperatures drop drastically after the sun sets. Few plants or animals can survive in this harsh **environment.**

Where in the World?

Mountains

Machu Picchu

Zones in the Himalaya

High Mountain Zone

Grasslands

Alpine Zone

Coniferous Forests

Temperate Forests

Tropical Forests

Traveling up the slope of the mountains, the temperature drops about 1°C (1.8°F) every 200 m (660 ft.), and rainfall increases. This creates a pattern of layered zones *(left)* that resembles the shift in climate regions as one travels from the **equator** toward the poles. Few creatures can live near the mountaintops, but in the Himalaya, butterflies are found at altitudes as high as 4,200 m (14,000 ft.).

Alpine Meadows

Above the tree line, alpine meadows bloom brightly in spring. Alpine plants grow low and close to the ground, like plants in the Arctic **tundra,** to survive harsh mountain conditions. Lower meadows make good pastures for dairy cattle. At high elevations some plants secrete a substance that makes them unpleasant to eat, so animals don't wander into this inhospitable zone.

Himalaya: On Top of the World

The world's eight tallest mountains lie in the Himalaya, whose name means "abode of the snow" in **Sanskrit.** That's appropriate, because most of the Himalaya's towering peaks are snowcapped and rise an average of 6,000 m (20,000 ft.) above sea level. Mount Everest, the tallest, is more than 8 km (5 mi.) above sea level. The Himalaya lie between India and China but also stretch across Pakistan, Nepal, Bhutan, and Tibet.

Living High

Mountain goats navigate high **terrain** with specially adapted hoofs that can dig into crevasses and give them traction in icy conditions. Shaggy fur coats insulate them against strong winds and low temperatures.

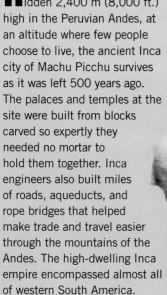

Hidden 2,400 m (8,000 ft.) high in the Peruvian Andes, at an altitude where few people choose to live, the ancient Inca city of Machu Picchu survives as it was left 500 years ago. The palaces and temples at the site were built from blocks carved so expertly they needed no mortar to hold them together. Inca engineers also built miles of roads, aqueducts, and rope bridges that helped make trade and travel easier through the mountains of the Andes. The high-dwelling Inca empire encompassed almost all of western South America.

Would You Believe?

Footprints from the Yeti

Is a hairy, humanlike yeti, or Abominable Snowman, roaming the Himalaya? Some people think this footprint belongs to the legendary beast. Others say this is a hoax, or just a bear track melting in the snow. What do you think?

Wetlands Damp and Wild

Swamp

W hether they are bogs, swamps, or marshes, wetlands are found where water meets the land. Covering about 6 percent of the earth's land surface, wetlands are among the world's richest **ecosystems.** Found in both salt- and freshwater **environments,** wetlands are home to many kinds of unusual trees and plants. They provide **habitats** and breeding grounds for a variety of migratory birds, fish, shellfish, and insects.

Wetlands are also valuable because they protect the land. Like giant sponges, wetlands absorb excess rainfall and melting snow, protecting drier areas from flooding. The thick vegetation acts as a filter, catching waste material and pollutants in its jumble of roots. This helps make the water cleaner as it passes through. Along coasts, marshes act as buffer zones that protect the fragile beaches from **erosion.**

Where in the World?

Wetlands

Knee-deep water floods a swamp in Louisiana filled with bald cypress trees. Swamps are heavily forested wetlands that are usually found at the edges of lakes and streams where drainage is poor.

Swamp Things

Gators

Tree's Knees

Alligators are the largest reptiles in North American swamps. The one above is sneaking up on its prey by submerging up to its eyes and breathing through its nose, hardly disturbing the water.

The knobby "knees" poking up from this swamp are part of the roots of cypress trees. Scientists think that because their roots lie underwater, the trees sprout knees to get oxygen from the air.

Marsh

Grasses dominate the landscape in marshes, which are found in low, flat areas in both salt- and freshwater environments.

River of Grass

Everglades National Park in southwestern Florida is a diverse wetlands ecosystem that is characterized by swamps, marshes, and pine **forests**. It is home to alligators, cougars, herons, and bald eagles. One of its special features is an 80-km (50-mi.)-wide, 160-km (100-mi.)-long "river of grass" *(left)*, a marshy environment dominated by sawgrass. Its average depth is only 15 cm (6 in.).

Bogs

The Danish farmer above is cutting peat from a bog. He will stack and dry the peat to burn as fuel for his stove. Bogs are found in cool **climates**. Their soft, spongy peat is formed as shallow lake beds fill up with decaying moss and other plant matter.

Strange But TRUE!

Bog Man

At first mistaken for a murder victim, this mummified body of a 2,000-year-old man was found in a Danish peat bog. The man was so well preserved that scientists could examine the lunch left in his stomach from the day he died.

The Dynamic Earth

A true view of the earth, as seen from space, shows the different **environments** that define the land of each **continent.**

The Rocky Mountains in North America and the Andes in South America rim the continents' western edge, giving way to plains and valleys that are drained by mighty **rivers,** such as the Mississippi in North America and the Amazon in South America.

Across the Atlantic Ocean lies the continent of Europe; its boundaries are fixed by the Mediterranean Sea in the south and Russia's Ural Mountains and the Caspian Sea in the east. Beyond this line begins Asia, covering one-third of the world's landmass. Here the snow-topped mountains of the Himalaya create a weather barrier that makes the south hot and humid and the north hot and dry, turning into cool forests and **tundra** farther north in Russia's Siberia.

Africa's great **desert** in the north and thick central jungles are sliced by the Great Rift Valley in the east, reaching from the Red Sea south to Lake Malawi.

The continents of Australia and Antarctica *(below)* lie separate from the others. Australia's fiercely hot desert spreads through its heartland, giving way to a **temperate** strip in the east and southeast.

Antarctica: At the Bottom

Rectangular maps like the one above right distort the shape of Antarctica *(bottom, in white),* which appears in its true form in the satellite image at left. The South Pole lies roughly in the center of this ice-covered land. The tip of the **peninsula,** at far left, stretches toward South America.

Faces of the World

Left: A girl from Germany
Below: Korean drummers

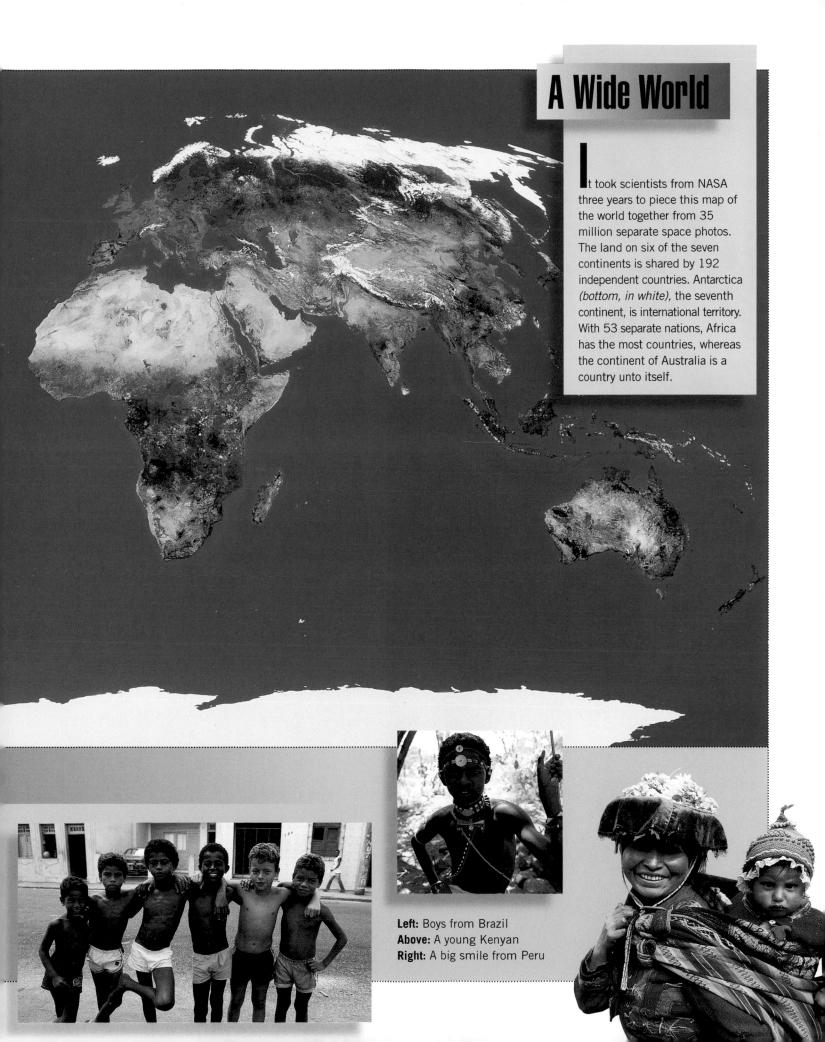

A Wide World

It took scientists from NASA three years to piece this map of the world together from 35 million separate space photos. The land on six of the seven continents is shared by 192 independent countries. Antarctica *(bottom, in white)*, the seventh continent, is international territory. With 53 separate nations, Africa has the most countries, whereas the continent of Australia is a country unto itself.

Left: Boys from Brazil
Above: A young Kenyan
Right: A big smile from Peru

North America

The **continent** of North America is made up of 10 countries. The three largest are Canada, the United States, and Mexico. Just south of Mexico are the other seven countries, and as a group they are known as Central America. North America also includes a number of **islands,** ranging in size from the small nations of the West Indies to Greenland, the biggest island in the world. (Greenland belongs to Denmark in Europe.)

The Rocky Mountains define the landscape in the West, stretching from Alaska down to Mexico. Fertile **plains** sweep through the middle of the continent, and thousands of lakes rim the Northeast, the largest of which are the Great Lakes.

Anthropologists—the scientists who study people and their customs—believe that the first humans to inhabit North America arrived about 16,000 years ago. They probably came from Asia, crossing into Alaska on a land bridge that once joined the two continents. They migrated to other areas, traveling as far south as South America to make their homes. Out of all the people who live in North America today, more than half live in the United States.

Mount McKinley

A mountain climber near the peak of Alaska's Mount McKinley (Denali) in Denali National Park pauses to take in the scenery. At 6,194 m (20,320 ft.), the mountain is the highest peak in North America. The upper portion of the mountain, which is part of the Alaska Range, is always covered in snow. The temperature on the summit can dip to -56°C (-70°F) in winter—and some climbers who have tried to reach the summit in those conditions have perished in the cold.

Fast FACTS

Area 24,256,000 sq km (9,366,000 sq mi.)

Population 470,000,000

Number of Independent Countries 23

Most Populous Countries
United States: 270,000,000
Mexico: 97,500,000

Most Populous Metropolitan Areas
Mexico City (Mexico): 19,000,000
New York (U.S.A.): 18,054,000
Los Angeles (U.S.A.): 13,471,000

Highest Mountains
Mount McKinley (Denali) (U.S.A.): 6,194 m (20,320 ft.)
Mount Logan (Canada): 5,951 m (19,524 ft.)

Longest Rivers
Mississippi-Missouri (U.S.A.): 6,019 km (3,740 mi.);
Mackenzie (Canada): 4,240 km (2,635 mi.);
Yukon (Canada): 3,184 km (1,979 mi.)

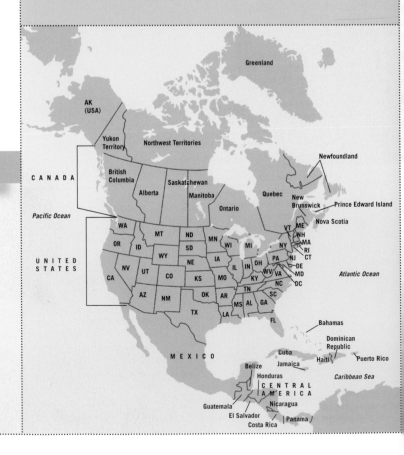

The View from Space

This satellite image of North America shows the ranges of the Rocky Mountains in the West in dark brown, followed by mottled brown deserts. Dark green represents **coniferous** forests in the North, edged by light brown tundra and white permanent ice. In the East are the green, fertile plains and **deciduous** forests.

Canada The Great White North

Grain silos like this one dot the midwestern prairie provinces of Manitoba, Saskatchewan, and Alberta. Farmers plant many kinds of grain, but wheat is the most important crop.

Canada is the second largest country in the world—only Russia is bigger. Yet for a large country, it is sparsely populated; in fact, the state of California has more people than Canada's 10 provinces and two territories put together. This is because much of Canada is extremely cold, and inhabited only by **indigenous** people who make their living hunting and fishing in the ice and snow. As a result, most of the country's major cities are located in the south. What Canada lacks in population, it makes up in **natural resources.** Along the coastlines there is abundant fishing, and the country's interior is rich in oil and minerals like copper, lead, and silver. Wheat and other grains grow on the southern **plains.** And the **forests** of the frigid north provide half of the paper on which the world's newspapers are printed.

Where in the World?

Canada

Gold Fever

In 1897, 100,000 prospectors loaded with tools and provisions trudged up the "Golden Stairs" —the chiseled ice steps of the Chilkoot Pass—hoping to find riches in the gold fields of northwest Canada's Yukon Territory. But gold fever could not keep the men warm when it got as cold as -62°C (-80°F) —and when they realized that few would get rich, because most of the gold lay in bedrock under 5 m (17 ft.) of frozen soil.

Would You Believe?

British Columbia

Settled by Canadian Indians, who recorded their history and traditions on totem poles *(right),* British Columbia is home to Vancouver, Canada's third largest city and the site of a busy port. Located on the Pacific **Ocean,** the southwestern province has a milder **climate** than anywhere else in Canada and has one of the country's longest growing seasons. Farming, commercial fishing, mining, and timber are its most lucrative **industries.**

Cowboys in Training

A bronco-busting teen takes a spill at the Little Britches Rodeo in Alberta, where wheat fields give way to cattle ranches and oil fields, and where the world's largest rodeo—the Calgary Stampede—takes place.

Quebec and Ontario

Ice skaters in the capital city of Ottawa glide along the Rideau Canal, past the turreted buildings of the Canadian Parliament on the left *(above)*. Located in Ontario, Canada's southern-most province, Ottawa sits roughly midway between Toronto, the country's largest city, and Montreal, about 193 km (120 mi.) to the east in Quebec. Settled in 1608 by the French, Quebec is the oldest of the provinces. Here people speak French. Most of the towns and the industry are concentrated along the St. Lawrence River, which is the outlet from the Great Lakes. Quebec's **rivers** and lakes provide it with nearly unlimited hydroelectric power.

The Northwest Territories

Below, an Inuit paddles a kayak in the sparsely populated North-west Territories, which accounts for one-third of Canada's land-mass. The government has returned much of the region to the Inuit, who call the area Nunavut, or "our land."

The Maritime Provinces

Lobster traps and fishing boats line the harbor at Salvage, one of the fishing villages on the Eastport Peninsula of Newfoundland. It is typical of the villages found in the other maritime provinces—Nova Scotia, New Brunswick, and Prince Edward **Island.**

The United States is not the largest country in the world or the most populous. But it is one of the wealthiest. This is because the United States has a vast supply of **natural resources** and a **climate** that allows for a long growing season. The farms of the Midwest produce so much food that there is more than enough for everyone in the United States. The differing climates across the country produce a wide array of crops—from oranges in Florida to winter wheat in North and South Dakota. Along the Gulf of Mexico in the south and Alaska in the far north, oil is a major **industry,** whereas coal mining ranks high in the north and west.

The country is diverse in another important way —its people. Because it was mostly settled by immigrants from other lands, it has been called a melting pot— where hundreds of different **cultures** meet and blend, creating a new culture.

Where in the World?

Alaska (USA)

Hawaii (USA)   United States

New England

Across the Northeast in the United States, towns like East Orange in Vermont blaze with colorful fall foliage. Called New England by early British colonists, the area includes Maine, New Hampshire, Vermont, Massachusetts, Rhode Island, and Connecticut.

New York, New York

Manhattan **Island** *(right)* is just one of the five boroughs that make up New York City, the largest city in the United States. Originally founded by the Dutch, who called it New Amsterdam, New York was the nation's capital before Washington, D.C. *(opposite),* was established. However, it remains the financial and cultural center of the United States.

The Southeast

The Capital City

Inside the U.S. Capitol building *(left)*, in the nation's capital city of Washington, D.C., members of the United States Congress make the country's laws. The city was established in 1790 on a 259-sq-km (100-sq-mi.) triangular patch of land carved from the states of Maryland and Virginia.

A Mix of Cultures

These high-school students from Annandale, Virginia, define the American concept of "melting pot." Students from more than 130 countries are enrolled in this school. Some of the nations they come from are the United States, Russia, the Ivory Coast, Ethiopia, Vietnam, Pakistan, Korea, Lebanon, and Peru.

The Oldest City

Where on EARTH?

St. Augustine, Florida, is the oldest continuously inhabited city in the United States—and the site of the oldest existing fort, the Castillo de San Marcos *(right)*, built in 1672. Explorer Juan Ponce de León first claimed the land in Florida in 1513; the city was officially founded in 1565.

United States of America

Named in honor of an Italian explorer *(below)*, America belonged to England when it declared its independence in 1776. The original 13 states grew in time to a total of 50, and today the United States also controls the territories of Puerto Rico, the Virgin Islands in the Caribbean Sea, and the **islands** of Guam and American Samoa in the Pacific Ocean.

Remarkable **geographic** features mark the land. Along the East Coast run the Appalachian Mountains, one of the oldest ranges on earth. In the upper Midwest, the Great Lakes—Michigan, Superior, Huron, Erie, and Ontario—form the world's largest source of fresh water. Between the Rocky Mountains and the Sierra Nevada lie Arizona's Grand Canyon *(right)* and a **desert** that includes Death Valley, where the temperature has hit a record 55°C (131°F). By contrast, in Mount Waialeale, Hawaii, the average annual rainfall of 11,500 mm (460 in.) makes it one of the wettest spots on earth.

More than 1.5 km (1 mi.) deep, the Grand Canyon stretches across northwestern Arizona for 350 km (217 mi.). It took six million years for the Colorado River to carve out this awesome gorge.

What's in a Name?

Naming America

Though Christopher Columbus was the first European explorer to visit the Americas, they were named in honor of Amerigo Vespucci, an Italian navigator who set sail for the New World in 1499. A cartographer, publishing an account of Vespucci's trip, suggested the land be called America, a Latin variation of the explorer's first name. The name stuck, and the **continents** of the New World became known as North and South America.

The Midwest—America's Heart

Cruising up the Mississippi River, an old-fashioned paddle-wheel boat passes the famous Gateway Arch that celebrates St. Louis's history as an important fur-trading post and the gateway to the West. The Mississippi, which flows from Minnesota to the Gulf of Mexico, is said to be the divide between the eastern and western states.

Hawaii, Raised by Volcanoes

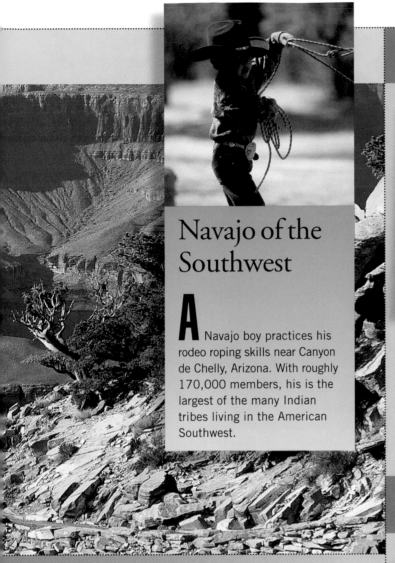

Navajo of the Southwest

A Navajo boy practices his rodeo roping skills near Canyon de Chelly, Arizona. With roughly 170,000 members, his is the largest of the many Indian tribes living in the American Southwest.

Fiery lava from Kilauea, the largest active volcano in the world, flows into the ocean off the coast of the "big island" of Hawaii. Eight major islands and 124 smaller ones make up the state of Hawaii, in the Pacific Ocean, nearly 3,800 km (2,400 mi.) west of San Francisco. The islands were formed at hot spots, where underwater volcanoes rose above sea level.

Alaska's Snaking Oil Pipe

The West Coast

From Washington State to Oregon and California, the Pacific Coast states are famous for vast forests and fruitful valleys. California, with its mild climate and long growing season, produces 20 percent (more than any other state) of America's fruit and vegetables, such as the pomegranates at left. The main agricultural region is the Central Valley, between the coastal mountain ranges and the Sierra Nevada, supported by irrigation from the San Joaquin and Sacramento Rivers.

An Alaskan and his dogsled swoosh alongside the pipeline that transports this state's rich oil reserves from oil fields near Prudhoe Bay in the north to the port of Valdez in the south, a journey of 1,280 km (800 mi.). The pipeline was completed in 1977, its construction spurred by the 1968 discovery of the largest petroleum deposits in North America.

Mexico Rich in History

W hen explorer Hernán Cortés, who conquered Mexico in the early 1500s, was asked by the king of Spain to describe the **terrain,** he is said to have crumpled a piece of paper and tossed it on the table. Those folds and creases represented Mexico's varied landscape: mountain ranges, **peninsulas,** stretches of **desert,** a high central **plateau,** coastal lowlands, **rain forests,** and active volcanoes.

Although much of the soil is poor, Mexican farms produce plenty of beans and corn, citrus fruit, mangoes, and melons, among other things. Large oil reserves fuel a growing petroleum **industry,** and minerals vital to technology—such as silver, copper, gold, lead, and iron—are found in abundance. Tourism is another source of income.

Where in the World?

Mexico

Mexico City

M exico City is the world's second largest city. This capital city lies in a high valley ringed by volcanoes, some of which are still active. Smog caused by fumes from cars and factories gets trapped by the **mountains** and hangs heavily over the city.

The Monarch Migration

Would You Believe?

Every fall, millions of monarch butterflies migrate from the U.S. and southern Canada— some traveling more than 3,200 km (2,000 mi.)—to winter in the **forests** west of Mexico City *(left).* In the spring they fly north and lay their eggs but do not live to a second winter.

Bringing Life to the Dead

On November 2—the Day of the Dead—Mexicans bring food and flowers to graveyards to honor loved ones. According to ancient belief, the dead can eat and hear on this day and visit with relatives. Children eat special sugar candy made in the shape of skulls.

Looking for a Nibble

With butterfly-shaped nets aboard, fishermen paddle along Lake Pátzcuaro, near Mexico's Pacific coast. Fishing is a way of life for those who live near the country's 10,000 km (6,000 mi.) of coastline, home to more than 100 different species of fish and shellfish.

Look Out Below!

Two children play among the ruins of the main temple of Chichén Itzá, a city built by Maya Indians in the sixth century. Located on the Yucatán Peninsula, the city grew up around two large wells in the seasonally dry region. Ancient Maya threw young people into a well to please their gods. These two had better watch out!

Mother Mountains

Running roughly parallel to Mexico's east and west coasts are two large mountain ranges— the Sierra Madre Oriental to the east and the Sierra Madre Occidental *(right)* to the west. Spanish for "mother mountains," the Sierra Madres are home to dense pine and oak forests. The mountain ranges converge near Mexico City.

Central America and the West Indies

Central America forms a land bridge, called an **isthmus,** that connects Mexico and South America. The region is made up of seven countries: Guatemala, Belize, Honduras, El Salvador, Nicaragua, Costa Rica, and Panama, with a population of 34.6 million. Shipping *(opposite, bottom right)* and agriculture are Panama's moneymakers; elsewhere in Central America the tropical **climate** and fertile soil support a wide range of crops, including bananas, coffee, and tobacco.

East of Central America lie the West Indies, volcanic **islands** that are home to nearly 37 million people—though 70 percent of them live in Cuba, Haiti, and the Dominican Republic. Spanish, French, British, and Dutch settlers colonized the islands, and African slaves worked the fields, which yielded such crops as bananas and sugarcane —still major exports today.

Where in the World?

Bahamas
Dominican Republic
Cuba
Belize
Honduras
Jamaica
Haiti
Puerto Rico
Guatemala
Nicaragua
El Salvador
Panama
Costa Rica

Columbus, Honorary Islander

Where on EARTH?

Christopher Columbus reached the New World in 1492, but it is unclear where he landed. Historians at first thought it was San Salvador, an island in the Bahamas where the cross at left stands. But evidence now points to a landing site at the nearby island of Samana Cay.

Cuba

When Cuba's sugarcane is ready to harvest, adults and children— who go to school half the day and tend crops the other half—work in the fields *(above)*. Cuba is the world's largest sugar exporter.

Central America

Guatemala

The ruins of the Temple of the Giant Jaguar, one of the many shrines of the ancient Maya city of Tikal, tower above the **rain forest** of northern Guatemala. Some 10 million people lived in the Maya lowlands in the ninth century. Modern Maya still thrive here.

The Dutch Touch

The architecture of these buildings in Willemstad, Curaçao, serves as a reminder that the "ABC" islands of the Netherlands Antilles—Aruba, Bonaire, and Curaçao—were once a Dutch colony. They lie off the coast of Venezuela.

Very British Islands

Once a hideout for Blackbeard and Captain Kidd, the islands of the British West Indies now harbor tourists—and locals who grow cotton, raise livestock, and relax by playing cricket *(right)*, the British version of baseball.

Barbados

At the eastern end of the Windward Islands lies Barbados. With its palm trees and sandy beaches Barbados is typical of the Caribbean vacationlands. Named by the Portuguese, who discovered the island, for "los barbados," the bearded fig trees, the island was later settled by the British. Among the early settlers was Sam Lord, a buccaneer who lured treasure ships to their doom in the outlying reefs by putting up lights, as if there were a harbor. Barbados achieved its independence in 1966, and instead of practicing piracy, people make their living from fishing, farming, refining sugarcane into molasses, and tourism.

Costa Rica—the Rich Coast

Columbus named Costa Rica the "rich coast" when he saw its people wearing fine gold jewelry. Although it mines no gold, Costa Rica treasures its rain forests, home to the white-faced capuchin monkeys below and more than 200 other mammal species.

Honduras

The poorest country in Central America and hit in 1998 by Hurricane Mitch, Honduras once produced one-third of the world's bananas. Bananas, coffee, and sugarcane are still exports.

Panama

At the narrowest point in Central America—only 50 km (30 mi.) across—ships traveling from the Atlantic to the Pacific Ocean pass through the Panama Canal. A series of locks raise and lower the ships to bring them level with the oceans as they cross. The canal was built by the U.S. and is operated by the U.S. until 2000, when Panama will assume control.

South America

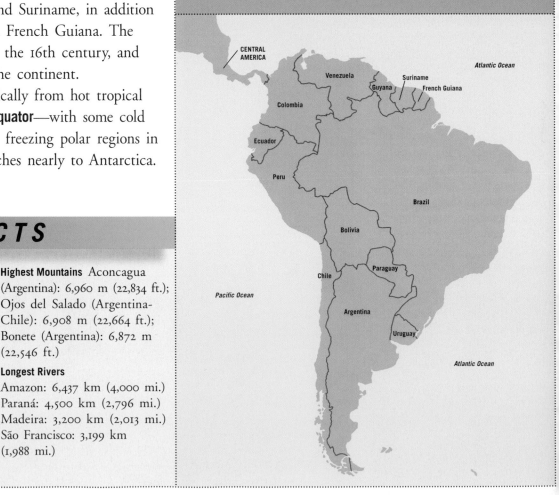

Where the land bridge that is Central America ends, South America begins. The fourth largest **continent** on earth, South America has **mountains, forests, plains,** and **deserts,** but it is dominated by two **geographic** features: the Andes Mountains and the Amazon **River.** Running the entire length of the continent, the Andes are the longest mountain range in the world and second in height only to the Himalaya in Asia. Many of the streams and rivers feed into the Amazon River *(top right),* which cuts across the continent through Brazil's Amazon Basin, the world's largest **rain forest.**

South America was originally inhabited by Indians. Today it is made up of 12 countries: Colombia, Peru, Venezuela, Ecuador, Bolivia, Chile, Argentina, Brazil, Uruguay, Paraguay, Guyana, and Suriname, in addition to a French **dependency** called French Guiana. The Portuguese colonized Brazil in the 16th century, and Spain dominated the rest of the continent.

The **climate** changes drastically from hot tropical zones in the north near the **equator**—with some cold spots at high **altitudes**—to the freezing polar regions in the south, where the land reaches nearly to Antarctica.

The Amazing Amazon

Deluged by an annual rainfall of 2,650 to 3,000 mm (106 to 120 in.), the Amazon River *(above)* empties 643 billion l (170 billion gal.) of water into the Atlantic Ocean every hour. The river starts in the Peruvian Andes and flows east through the Amazon Basin—an area that accounts for nearly 40 percent of Brazil's landmass. The rain forest and its rivers nurture several million plant and animal species—more than half of all those on earth.

Fast FACTS

Area 17,819,000 sq km (6,880,454 sq mi.)

Population 331,000,000

Number of Independent Countries 12

Most Populous Countries
Brazil: 162,100,000
Argentina: 36,000,000

Most Populous Cities
São Paulo, Brazil: 15,784,888
Rio de Janeiro, Brazil: 10,489,000
Buenos Aires, Argentina: 9,968,000

Highest Mountains Aconcagua (Argentina): 6,960 m (22,834 ft.); Ojos del Salado (Argentina-Chile): 6,908 m (22,664 ft.); Bonete (Argentina): 6,872 m (22,546 ft.)

Longest Rivers
Amazon: 6,437 km (4,000 mi.)
Paraná: 4,500 km (2,796 mi.)
Madeira: 3,200 km (2,013 mi.)
São Francisco: 3,199 km (1,988 mi.)

Rain Forests, Mountains, and Deserts

In this colorized satellite image of South America, the green expanse cutting across the continent is the Amazon Basin, with its vast rain forests. Along the west coast the snow-capped Andes Mountains reach north to south, and **grasslands** cover the brown areas.

Riches in Northern South America

Colombia

S cratch the soil of the northernmost countries in South America—Colombia, Venezuela, Guyana, Suriname, and the **dependency** of French Guiana—and you'll most likely find riches. Colombia is bursting with deposits of gold, coal, and the beautiful green stones called emeralds. Neighboring Venezuela is one of the world's largest oil producers, and the smaller regions of Guyana, Suriname, and French Guiana cut timber from **rain forests;** mine bauxite, which is processed into aluminum; and farm. The Indian word Guiana means "land of waters," and in the humid lowlands along the Atlantic coast, fertile farmland produces rice and sugarcane.

In Colombia and Venezuela, land that was once used for farming and ranching is increasingly being drilled for oil. Today, only about 25 percent of all South Americans still work in agriculture.

Behind the walls of San Felipe de Barajas, a 16th-century fort, the modern city of Cartagena sprawls over a **peninsula** and three **islands** along the Caribbean coast. It is Colombia's chief port for exporting oil, platinum, and coffee. Colombia also has a coastline along the Pacific.

Where in the World?

Venezuela · Guyana · Suriname · French Guiana · Colombia

Would You *Believe?*

Monster Gems

Colombian mines produce about 90 percent of the world's emeralds. This green giant weighs more than 340 g (12 oz.).

Cleared for Takeoff

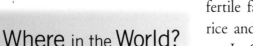

L ocated in Kourou, French Guiana, the Guiana Space Center is the launching pad for the European Space Agency's satellites. French Guiana, a French dependency, is a better site for a space center than any place in Europe because the country is located near the **equator.** There, the earth spins faster than anywhere else, giving rockets an extra lift.

Coffee Crop

Workers pick coffee beans at a plantation in the Colombian highlands, where growing conditions are ideal. Making up about half of the country's exports, the beans are harvested when they are red green, then roasted to a dark brown to bring out their flavor.

Venezuela

Mountains in the Clouds

Mount Roraima *(left)* is just one of many tepuis, or flat-topped mountains, that rise above the clouds in northern Venezuela. Formed as the Orinoco River and its **tributaries** eroded the surrounding rock, the tepuis are home to many rare species of plants and animals.

Oil on Water

Thousands of oil derricks rise from the water and line the shores of Venezuela's Lake Maracaibo *(left),* pumping petroleum through underwater pipelines to storage tanks on land. Responsible for about two-thirds of the country's total petroleum output, Lake Maracaibo—actually an inlet of the Gulf of Venezuela—flows over the top of one of the world's richest oil fields.

Angel Falls

Adventurers with parachutes strapped to their backs leap from the top of Angel Falls, which have a vertical drop of 979 m (3,212 ft.). Angel Falls, the world's highest waterfall, are part of the Churún **River** in Venezuela and drop from a flat-topped tepui known as Devil's **Mountain.** The waterfall is named for James Angel, an American who crash-landed his airplane there in 1937.

Diversity in Peru, Bolivia, and Ecuador

For the South American countries of Ecuador, Peru, and Bolivia, the Andes Mountains define the work people do. In Ecuador—named for the **equator,** which passes through the country —the mountains form a distinct dividing line. West of the Andes is a fertile, low-lying coastal area where coffee, bananas, and other crops grow, and to the east lie tropical **forests** and oil-rich lands. The mountain highlands are home to the Quechua Indians, who farm and weave brightly colored textiles. Quito, Ecuador's capital, is located there as well.

As the Andes wind farther south through Peru and Bolivia they split into two parallel ranges; in between is the **altiplano,** an area of high **plateaus** with an average elevation of 3.2 km (2 mi.). The people who live there have developed extra-large lungs to help them breathe more efficiently.

Where in the World?

Bolivia

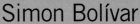
Lake Titicaca

Guiding a boat made of bundled totora reeds, an Indian glides across Lake Titicaca. The lake sits on the altiplano astride the border of Bolivia and Peru, and at 8,300 sq km (3,200 sq mi.) is the second largest in South America. Forty-one **islands,** some densely populated, dot the lake.

What's in a Name?

Simon Bolívar

Simon Bolívar (1783-1830), a Venezuelan statesman, led the fight to free much of South America from Spanish rule. In 1825, a newly liberated country near Peru was named Bolivia in his honor.

A herd of young llamas graze in the arid highlands of Peru. Llamas are the pack animals of the Andes, carrying heavy loads across high mountain passes. Along with their relatives the alpacas, the guanacos, and the vicunas, llamas also provide meat, milk, and thick wool that is woven into clothing. All are related to the camel.

Peru

Source of the Amazon

Though most of the Amazon River winds through the steamy Brazilian **rain forest,** the river gets its start in the frigid Peruvian Andes. One of the river's sources is the glacier below. As the glacier melts, water flows down the mountains to form streams. They meet up with other **tributaries,** and then combine to form one of the largest rivers in the world.

The Maiden in the Ice

A climber on a mountain peak in the Peruvian Andes recovers the mummified remains of a teenager. The girl had been sacrificed to Inca gods about 500 years ago. Discovered in 1995, the mummy had been enclosed in ice until an avalanche sent her sliding down the slope.

Ecuador, Wearing the Equator as a Belt

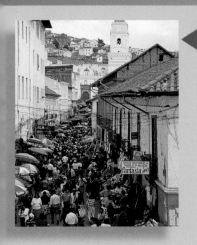

Quito, Ecuador

Stalls selling Indian crafts and foods line the streets of Quito, the capital of Ecuador. Foods for sale include potatoes, maize, and tomatoes, which originated in South America. Quito, the oldest capital city in South America, was founded in 1534 by the Spanish, whose influence can still be seen in its architecture.

The Galápagos

A land iguana at the edge of a volcanic crater on the Galápagos Islands seeks a path to its nest. About 1,000 km (600 mi.) west of Ecuador and belonging to it, the Galápagos were formed by underwater volcanoes. They were discovered by a Spanish explorer in 1535. Most of the land is now a wildlife park.

Brazil Paraguay, & Uruguay

With an area of more than 8.5 million sq km (3 million sq mi.), Brazil is the largest country in South America. Its dominant feature is the Amazon Basin, a huge expanse of **rivers** and tropical **rain forest** that provides lumber and latex—for rubber and also as an ingredient in chewing gum—among other **natural resources.** Brazil's fertile soil grows one-third of the world's coffee supply, as well as sugarcane, tropical fruits, and cacao, from which chocolate is made. In an effort to create new farmland, Brazilians have been clearing sections of the rain forest, which has resulted in the loss of some plant and animal species.

South of Brazil lie two smaller countries: Paraguay and Uruguay. Paraguay generates more than half its income from the sale of hydroelectric power to Brazil. Much of the land in both countries is used for cattle herding.

Where in the World?

Brazil

Paraguay

Uruguay

Paraguay

A man carries reeds cut from the shores of Lake Ypacaraí in south-central Paraguay. The nearby Paraguay River divides the country roughly in half. Most people live on the east side of the river.

Uruguay

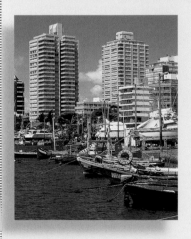

The modern resort of Punta del Este in Uruguay, 113 km (70 mi.) east of the capital city of Montevideo on the Atlantic coast, shows little of the country's rural side. Millions of cattle and sheep graze in the low, rolling **grasslands** of the country's interior. The livestock provides beef and wool for export.

Tropical Paradise

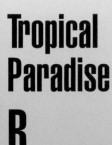

Rio de Janeiro *(below)* is a spectacular tourist spot and a major port city. The Portuguese navigators who discovered it on January 1, 1502, thought it lay at the mouth of a river, hence they gave it the name "January River."

Join the Carnival!

This gaily dressed woman joins others celebrating Rio de Janeiro's yearly carnival. Taking place just before Lent, 40 days during which Roman Catholics traditionally avoid eating meat, the carnival includes parades and costume balls.

Then & NOW!

Brasília

In a move designed to boost development of the country's vast interior, Brazilian officials ordered tracts of rain forest land cleared for a new capital city *(far left)*. In 1960, the federal government moved into the gleaming modern buildings of the brand-new city of Brasília *(inset)*, more than 500 miles inland from Rio de Janeiro.

Life in the Rain Forest

Instead of a line and hook, the Indian above uses a bow and arrow to hunt for fish in an Amazon Basin river. The rain forest is home to more than 100,000 Indians who fish and hunt for their food and depend entirely on the **forest** for their every need.

Contrasts in Argentina and Chile

In the southern portion of South America the Andes Mountains form the border between the area's two largest countries: Argentina to the east and Chile to the west. Both countries enjoy rich mineral deposits, such as oil, natural gas, and coal in Argentina, and copper and iron ore in Chile *(opposite, far right)*. The landscapes vary from **rain forest** to **desert** to grassy **plains** where cattle graze *(below)*.

Chile—which means "where the land ends"—isn't named for a long, skinny chili pepper, even though it looks like one. The country is 4,260 km (2,650 mi.) long but only 400 km (250 mi.) across at its widest point. The southern tip is among the wettest, stormiest places on earth, whereas the northern end is home to the Atacama Desert, where some areas go hundreds of years without a drop of rain. Most people live in the mild central region.

Where in the World?

Buenos Aires

High-rise buildings spike the skyline of Buenos Aires, the capital of Argentina and its largest city. One of the world's major ports, the city bustles with industry—manufacturing, food processing, metalworking, and auto assembly.

The Pampas of Argentina

Gauchos, or cowboys, lead cattle to fresh pastures in the **grasslands** of Argentina. Called the **pampas**, the vast plain stretches from east to west across much of central Argentina. Sheep and cattle are bred in the cooler southeast; crops are raised in the western area.

Tierra del Fuego—Land of Fire

When Ferdinand Magellan sailed around South America's tip in 1520, he saw campfires on the coast. But the land he named Tierra del Fuego—Land of Fire—is mostly covered with glaciers. Part of the **island** chain belongs to Argentina and the rest to Chile.

In central Chile's scenic lake district resort area, Lake Llanquihue and the town of Puerto Varas sit in the shadow of Osorno Volcano, part of the Andes Mountains.

Mining Chile

Even the biggest dump trucks look like toys in Chile's huge Chuquicamata copper mine *(above),* the largest in the world. Chile produces more copper than any other country, and the metal accounts for 40 percent of its exports. Among other valuable metals and minerals dug from the land are gold, silver, lead, and nitrates, which are used for fertilizer.

Chile's mineral wealth is concentrated in the northern part of the country, in the Atacama Desert. So valuable are the minerals mined there that Chile, Bolivia, and Peru fought a war from 1879 to 1883 for control of the area.

Where on EARTH?

Easter Island

More than 600 stone statues like the ones at left—some of which are 12 m (40 ft.) high— are scattered across Easter Island. The island, which lies 3,780 km (2,350 mi.) west of Chile, was colonized in about the year 400 by Polynesians. Competing clans are thought to have carved the statues. The island was annexed by Chile in 1888, and declared a national park in 1935.

Golden Era of the Inca

The Inca empire—ranging from Ecuador south to central Chile *(yellow on map)*—fell to the Spanish in 1532. Gold objects beautifully crafted by the Indians were melted down and taken to Spain. The birds below are among the few remaining treasures.

Europe Small and Scenic

Europe is the jagged, eastern end of Eurasia, the landmass that also includes Asia. It is less than half the size of North America, making it one of the smallest **continents.** Yet Europe is densely populated; only Asia has more people.

You could stand anywhere in western Europe and be no more than 480 km (300 mi.) from the sea. It's not surprising, then, that fishing and sailing have played a big role in these people's lives. Sometimes the oldest cities were built near ports, as was the case in Athens, Greece, and Rome, Italy. Sometimes they were built alongside **rivers,** as in Vienna, Austria (on the Danube), Cologne, Germany (on the Rhine), Paris, France (on the Seine), or London, England (on the Thames).

For centuries, high **mountain** ranges, including the Pyrenees, the Alps, the Caucasus, and the Balkans, kept people isolated from each other, so they developed many different **cultures** and more than 40 languages. Lately, the people of Europe have set aside their differences and begun working together on economic and other issues.

A Sky-High View

Much of Europe's 80,000 km (50,000 mi.) of coastline can be seen in this satellite photo. The north is dominated by Scandinavia's craggy shape, and the south shows the distinct boot shape of Italy reaching toward Africa.

Iceland · Norway · Finland · Baltic Sea · Atlantic Ocean · Sweden · Estonia · Russia · North Sea · Latvia · Ireland · Netherlands · Denmark · Lithuania · Russia · United Kingdom · Belarus · Luxembourg · Belgium · Germany · Poland · Liechtenstein · Switzerland · Czech Republic · Ukraine · Slovakia · France · Austria · Hungary · Moldova · Italy · Croatia · Romania · Portugal · Slovenia · Monaco · San Marino · Black Sea · Spain · Andorra · Vatican City · Bulgaria · Greece · Bosnia and Herzegovina · Yugoslavia · Albania · Macedonia · Mediterranean Sea

Mont Blanc

Some people consider France's Mont Blanc *(above)*, which is 4,807 m (15,771 ft.) tall, the highest mountain in Europe. Others say that title belongs to Russia's Mount Elbrus near the Georgian border; its peak rises to 5,642 m (18,510 ft.). Which group is right? It depends on where the boundary line between Europe and Asia is drawn!

Fast FACTS

Area 10,530,750 sq km (4,066,241 sq mi.)

Population 728,000,000

Number of Independent Countries 42

Most Populous Countries
European Russia: 147,000,000
Germany: 82,000,000

Least Populous Country
Vatican City: 830

Most Populous Metropolitan Areas
London (England): 10,570,000
Moscow (Russia): 9,390,000
Paris (France): 8,510,000

Longest Rivers
Volga: 3,531 km (2,194 mi.)
Danube: 2,858 km (1,776 mi.)
Ural: 2,400 km (1,500 mi.)

The British Isles

The two main **islands** off the northwestern coast of Europe are Great Britain and Ireland. These islands are divided into two countries, the United Kingdom and the Republic of Ireland. The United Kingdom was formed in 1801. It consists of England, Wales, Scotland, and Northern Ireland. The Republic of Ireland was also part of the United Kingdom until it gained its independence in 1921.

Mountains and **hills** stretch along the northwestern shores of both islands, giving way to wide valleys and **plains** to the east. Warm winds from the Atlantic Ocean keep the **climate** mild and wet—great for farming. Today, however, most British and Irish people make their living in towns and cities, working in the textile, steel, banking, and computer **industries.**

Where in the World?

Britain's Coast

Britain has more than 5,000 km (3,000 mi.) of coastline. Much of it is rocky, with tall, magnificent cliffs. The white cliffs of Dover *(above)* can be seen by approaching ships from miles away. Britain is surrounded by the sea, and its people have been great fishermen and sailors. During the 18th and 19th centuries, the British navy was the most powerful fleet in the world. Its ships sailed around the world, creating an overseas empire that included such distant places as India, Australia, and North America.

Ireland: The Emerald Isle

Ireland is sometimes called the Emerald Isle because of its lush, green countryside. The land is so fertile because it is fed from below by a mineral-rich layer of limestone and from above by frequent rain showers. Ireland's green fields make it a great place to raise sheep. Sweaters made from Irish wool are worn around the world.

Would **You** *Believe?*

Blarney Stone

Holding iron bars for support, a visitor to Ireland's Blarney Castle leans back to kiss the famous Blarney Stone in the parapet. According to Irish folklore, whoever kisses the stone will become a great storyteller.

King Arthur's Camelot

According to ancient legend, England once had a king named Arthur who lived in a magical and mysterious land called Camelot. In the 15th-century drawing above, Arthur is shown returning with his knights to his castle in Camelot. Some people believe that the castle once stood in Cornwall in the rolling hills of southwestern England *(right)*.

Trudy Ederle

On August 6, 1926, a 19-year-old American, Gertrude "Trudy" Ederle, became the first woman to swim 56 km (35 mi.) across the English Channel. She swam from France to England in 14 hours and 31 minutes—two hours faster than any man had swum it before her. This amazing feat made her world famous.

The Mysterious Loch Ness

Scotland is dotted with lakes that were carved out by glaciers some 20,000 years ago during the last **Ice Age.** The largest of these lakes is Loch Ness. (*Loch* means "lake.")

Long and very narrow, Loch Ness's cold, murky waters are more than 200 m (700 ft.) deep. Some people believe a reptile-like monster lives in the lake. A few claim to have seen or even photographed it *(below)!* Others think such sightings are a hoax.

London

London, the largest city in the British Isles and the capital of the United Kingdom, was founded in AD 43 by Roman invaders. For its first 1,000 years London grew slowly, but with the arrival of William the Conqueror in 1066 the city began its rise to fame. Today, more than 10 million people live there, including the queen of England and her family. London is located near the **mouth** of the Thames **River,** the longest river in Britain. The city has many splendid buildings, including the Clock Tower *(right)*, which houses a huge bell called Big Ben. The tower is part of the Houses of Parliament, where Britain's elected officials meet to pass laws.

Scandinavia & Baltic States

Scandinavia is a name **geographers** have given the northernmost countries of Europe—Sweden, Norway, Denmark, Finland, and Iceland. All share similar **cultures** and histories. In the Middle Ages they were the home of the Vikings, seafarers who raided coastal towns and villages throughout Europe.

Much of Scandinavia is rugged and mountainous. Iceland has 200 active volcanoes; at least one erupts every five years. Denmark, however, is flat and marshy. It is made up of one large **peninsula** and almost 500 **islands,** which are connected by bridges and ferries. Greenland, in North America, belongs to Denmark as well and has a population of 55,000.

Across the Baltic Sea lie the Baltic States: Latvia, Lithuania, and Estonia. These small countries were variously invaded by the Danes, Germans, Swedes, Poles, and Russians but now are independent.

Where in the World?

Where on EARTH?

Legoland Park

The popular Lego toy bricks were invented in Billund, Denmark, in the 1960s. Today, tourists to Billund can visit Legoland Park, where almost everything is built out of them, including the boat at left.

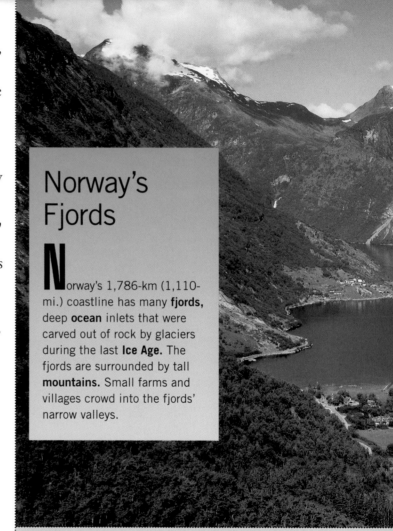

Norway's Fjords

Norway's 1,786-km (1,110-mi.) coastline has many **fjords,** deep **ocean** inlets that were carved out of rock by glaciers during the last **Ice Age.** The fjords are surrounded by tall **mountains.** Small farms and villages crowd into the fjords' narrow valleys.

Iceland

Iceland is an island lying 1,000 km (600 mi.) west of Norway, just below the **Arctic Circle.** Because it is so far north, Iceland has daylight for 24 hours during midsummer and darkness for most of the day during midwinter. Much of Iceland's soil is permanently frozen. Most people live in modern houses. The old, sod-covered farm dwellings at left are preserved as historic monuments today.

Baltic States

Lithuania

Lithuania is the largest of the Baltic States. It is a flat, low country with more than 800 **rivers** and 3,000 lakes and reservoirs. Lithuania's capital, Vilnius, dates back to the 14th century, when the country was more powerful and extended from the Baltic to the Black Sea.

Latvia

Every summer thousands of Latvians dressed in folk costumes gather in their capital city of Riga for a music festival *(left)*. This second largest Baltic State is a low-lying country with 4,000 lakes and large forests but is also heavily industrialized.

Estonia

The church spires of Talinn, the capital of Estonia, show its Nordic and Russian influence. The country, which includes about 800 islands in the Baltic Sea, is closely related to Finland.

Island City

Stockholm, Sweden's largest city and capital, lies on the coast of the Baltic Sea. It is made up of 14 small islands connected by 50 bridges. Stockholm is more than 700 years old. It grew from a small trading port to one of Europe's major cities. One of every six Swedes lives in Stockholm.

The Heart of Europe

Western Europe holds most of the **continent's** wealthy, industrial nations. France and Germany are the leaders, their northern plains thriving with productive farmland, giving way to important seaports, and their **industries** excelling with modern technology. Europe's tallest **mountains**—the Alps—shape the countries of Austria, Liechtenstein, and Switzerland. Many of Europe's famous **rivers,** including the Rhône in France and the Rhine in Germany—one of the world's busiest commercial waterways—flow from these mountains. Three small countries—the Netherlands, Belgium, and Luxembourg—are known as the Low Countries. Much of their land is flat and low-lying. In fact, half of the Netherlands is below sea level. The people who live there, called the Dutch, have built dikes to keep the sea out.

Where in the World?

Netherlands
Belgium
Luxembourg
Germany
Atlantic Ocean
France
Austria
Switzerland Liechtenstein
Monaco

A City on Stilts

Would You Believe?

Ice skaters stroll across a frozen canal in Amsterdam. The city, the Netherlands' capital, has 160 canals and hundreds of bridges and it is built on pilings—long wood and steel columns that keep the buildings from sinking into the swampy land.

France

France is the biggest country in western Europe. It also has the greatest variety of landscapes, and 3,200 km (2,000 mi.) of coastal beaches. Most people live in towns or cities, but farming is an important part of the **economy.** France produces more food than any other country in Europe, from artichokes to zucchini, and more than 300 kinds of cheeses. It is especially famous for its vineyards *(above)* and the wines that are made from those grapes.

City of Lights

Paris, on the Seine River, is the capital of France. It is well known for its broad boulevards and sidewalk cafés. Many of the buildings, like the Eiffel Tower *(right)*, are brightly lighted at night. That's why it is called the City of Lights.

A Country Reunited

Austria

For much of its history, Germany consisted of loosely united states, becoming one country in 1871. After World War II it was divided into the Federal Republic of Germany in the west and the German Democratic Republic under Communist rule in the east. They were reunited in 1990. Although Germany has many beautiful old buildings, such as these 16th-century houses in Bacharach, it is Europe's leading industrial country.

Three-quarters of Austria is in the snowcapped Alps. The country's spectacular scenery, such as that at Hallstätter Lake *(above)*, attracts tourists from around the world. Austria has strict laws that protect its mountains from overdevelopment and pollution.

Switzerland

Switzerland is a mostly mountainous country. Snowboarding and skiing are favorite winter activities. St. Bernard dogs *(below)* were once used to rescue lost hikers or injured skiers in the Swiss Alps. The dogs saved more than 2,500 people during 300 years of service. Rescuers now use helicopters.

What's a Euro?

The Euro is a new currency, like the U.S. dollar and the Japanese yen. Used by banks since 1999, the Euro will be in circulation as regular money by 2002 in the following countries: Germany, Belgium, Finland, France, Ireland, Italy, Luxembourg, the Netherlands, Austria, Portugal, and Spain. They hope this measure will unite them economically as one country.

Southern Europe

Southern Europe is divided from the rest of the **continent** by rugged **mountains** that include the Pyrenees, the Alps, and the Balkans. The three great **peninsulas** jutting into the Mediterranean Sea are homes to Portugal and Spain, Italy, and Greece. Much of these people's lives is centered on the Mediterranean, which leads to the Atlantic Ocean through the narrow Strait of Gibraltar.

Southern European winters are generally mild and wet. The summers are hot, dry, and sunny. This **climate** is great for growing olives, citrus fruits, nuts, and grapes. In Spain and Portugal, people also grow evergreen oak trees. The bark of the trees is dried and made into corks.

The ancient Greeks and the Romans, from Italy, once ruled over much of southern Europe. Many of their buildings and bridges are still standing 2,000 years later!

Where in the World?

Atlantic Ocean

Portugal
Spain
Andorra
Italy
Vatican City
Greece
Mediterranean Sea

Mysterious Basques

The Basque people live in a rugged area of northern Spain and southern France. But they are not really Spanish nor French. Their language is unlike any in Europe. In fact, the Basque language, Euskera, is not related to any other language in the world. No one knows where the Basque people came from, but they have probably lived in their current homeland as shepherds and farmers for at least 5,000 years. That makes them the oldest **ethnic** group in Europe.

Spain: Running with Bulls

Hundreds of people take part in the *encierro,* or running, of the bulls, in Pamplona, Spain, each July. The event is part of the town's Fiesta de San Fermín. Armed only with rolled-up newspapers, the runners try to keep ahead of the bulls as the animals charge from their pens to a nearby bullring, spearing anyone in their way.

Portugal's Life by the Sea

Fishermen ready their boat along Portugal's Atlantic coast. Portugal is a big exporter of seafood, especially tuna and sardines. The country has a long seafaring history. During the 15th and 16th centuries, Portuguese explorers discovered unknown parts of the world for Europe and established colonies in Africa, India, and South America.

Italy: Surrounded by the Sea

The **island** city of Venice *(right)* is but one of many important ports in Italy. The country's position in the middle of the Mediterranean enabled it to trade with the world. Venice was the main link between Europe and Asia. The city, built on more than 100 islands, has canals instead of streets. People get around Venice on foot or by boat.

How Small?

Vatican City

It's the smallest country in the world and is home to the pope, the head of the Roman Catholic Church. The city of Rome, Italy, surrounds it.

Greece: An Island Nation

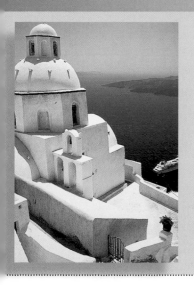

Greece, located at the southern end of the Balkan Peninsula, has more than 1,400 islands. Many towns rise steeply from the sea on the numerous mountains. Traditional houses and churches like this one in Thíra have thick walls and small windows to keep out the heat. The **culture** of ancient Greece—more than 2,500 years old—has influenced all of European civilization.

Tuscany's Vineyards

The hills of Tuscany *(above)* in northwest Italy are an extension of the Apennines, a mountain chain stretching the peninsula's length. Here grow Italy's famous vineyards, olive groves, and orchards.

Central and Eastern Europe

The vast region known as Central and Eastern Europe has high forested **mountains,** rugged **hills,** and flat farmland. Its **rivers** include the Vistula in the north and the Danube in the south. Some of its countries, such as Hungary and the Czech Republic, are landlocked. Others adjoin the Baltic, Adriatic, Ionian, or Black Seas.

Through the centuries, the many different **ethnic** groups of Central and Eastern Europe have waged fierce wars over how their countries should be divided. After World War II, Communist governments took over all of the region. When Communism began to collapse in 1989, new, independent and democratically elected countries formed amid new fighting. Some of the former Yugoslavia is now split up into the four new countries of Croatia, Slovenia, Bosnia-Herzegovina, and Macedonia.

Where in the World?

On the smaller farms in the foothills of the High Tatra Mountains in southern Poland, farmers often use horses instead of tractors to work the fields.

Would **You** *Believe?*

The novel *Dracula* is inspired by 15th-century Prince Vlad III, who lived in the castle at left in a region of Romania called Transylvania. The prince was nicknamed the Impaler because he had his enemies impaled on sharpened stakes.

Dracula's Castle

Romania

Romania is famous for its 500-year-old monasteries. Their outside walls are covered with beautiful paintings, such as those of the Sucevita Monastery (*above*) in northeast Romania.

Hungary on the Danube

Hungary's largest city and capital is Budapest *(above)*, formed by the cities of Buda and Pest on either side of the Danube River. Like the city, Hungary's great **plains** are also split in half by the mighty Danube. Since ancient times the Danube has given Hungary a link to the countries of western Europe and those of eastern Europe, where the river empties into the Black Sea. Hungary's fertile plains provide ample grain, potatoes, and vegetables, as well as orchards, vineyards, and grazing land for sheep and cattle.

Magyars, **nomads** who came from the east, settled Hungary in the ninth century and gave the country its distinct language, which is related to Finnish.

Bulgarian Oil

Most of the rose oil used in perfumes comes from flower fields in Bulgaria. Roses are harvested each June *(above)*, picked before 10:00 a.m. to retain their fragrance.

A Bridge to Peace

A boy dives from the ruins of the Stari Most Bridge in the city of Mostar, Bosnia-Herzegovina. The 400-year-old bridge was destroyed in 1993 when the country's Christian Serbs and Muslim Bosnians began fighting each other. Plans are now under way to rebuild the bridge as a symbol of peace.

On Croatia's Dalmatian Coast

The city of Dubrovnik *(right)* in the newly independent country of Croatia is more than 1,300 years old. It was built on a small island in the Adriatic Sea that is now connected to the mainland, where the Dinaric Alps rise behind it. This coastal region is known as Dalmatia and is the part of the world where Dalmatians *(right)* come from, which is how the dogs got their name.

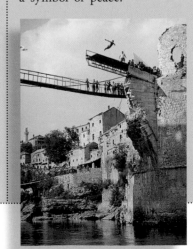

Russia and Its Neighbors

Russia, the world's biggest country, lies in both Asia and Europe. **Geographers** use the Ural **Mountains** as the dividing line between European and Asian Russia. About one-fourth of Russia's land is in Europe, an area of mostly treeless **plains** called **steppes** and a northern belt of **coniferous forests**. Russia's capital, Moscow, lies roughly in the center. Some nine million people live in Moscow, making it one of the largest cities in the world.

For centuries, Russia was ruled by emperors called tsars. After a revolution in 1917, it became a republic, governed by Communist leaders, who absorbed its neighbors into the Union of Soviet Socialist Republics (USSR). In 1991, Russia and the others became independent republics. Russia has joined with Ukraine and Belarus in Europe and other neighbors in Asia to form the Commonwealth of Independent States.

Where in the World?

End of Communism

A broken statue of Communist leader Joseph Stalin lies in a Moscow park. After the Communist Party lost power in 1991, Russians knocked down hundreds of memorials to Communist leaders.

Would You Believe?

Brrrrrrr!

A young member of a Russian "walrus club" dives into the icy water to test his courage in celebration of winter. The air temperature is -15°C (5°F) and the water temperature is about 1°C (33°F)—a typical December day.

A Historic Fortress

Moscow dates back to the 12th century. The city grew around a fortress called the Kremlin. Inside the Kremlin's walls are a grand palace, four cathedrals, and a church. The 500-year-old Bell Tower of Ivan the Great is the Kremlin's tallest structure.

Ukraine

Bedecked with fancy bows and white pinafores, Ukrainian schoolgirls bring flowers to their teacher on the first day of school.

Ukraine was annexed by Russia in the 18th century, to gain its freedom only in 1991. Its fertile steppe is one of the major wheat-producing areas of Europe, reaching from the borders of Poland and Belarus to the Black Sea.

The Urals: Where Europe Ends

A village in the foothills of Russia's Ural Mountains *(left)* is one of the last outposts of Europe. Beyond the mountains Asia begins. Extending for 2,400 km (1,500 mi.) north and south from the Arctic **tundra** to the **deserts** near the Caspian Sea, the Ural Mountains are covered with dense forests. Here **industry** is concentrated on lumber products and mining.

Black Sea

The Black Sea, with its tropical **climate** and white beaches, is a favorite vacation area. This inland sea between Europe and Asia is shared by six nations and joins the Mediterranean.

Asia Land of Extremes

What is made up of 46 countries, is home to both the highest and lowest points on earth, and has some of the hottest, coldest, wettest, and driest places in the world? The answer is Asia, the largest **continent** on the planet. Asia takes up nearly one-third of the earth's land surface, stretching from the north above the **Arctic Circle** to south below the **equator,** and east from the Ural Mountains of Europe and the Caspian Sea to within 88 km (55 mi.) of Alaska's Seward Peninsula of North America.

Vast **deserts** cover the Arabian Peninsula, as well as sections of China and central Asia, whereas Southeast Asia boasts the world's densest tropical forests. Few people live in the deserts or frozen wastes of northern Siberia, yet Asia has the largest population in the world: About six out of every 10 people on earth live there.

Although many of the countries—and the people who live in them—are poor, the continent has valuable **natural resources.** And more and more countries in Asia are following Japan's example and are developing a modern industrialized **economy.**

The Rice Bowl

Flooded rice fields hand carved into the hillsides in Indonesia are creating swirling, stairstepping patterns. This farming technique, called terracing, allows crops to be planted in mountainous regions. Rice is the most important crop in Asia and is a **staple** of the diet. Of the 10 percent of Indonesia's land that can be farmed, for example, most of it is devoted to rice. China, India, and Indonesia, in that order, are the world's top three rice producers.

Fast FACTS

Area 44,579,000 sq km (17,213,298 sq mi.)

Population 3,604,000,000

Most Populous Countries China: 1,249,200,000; India: 988,700,000

Most Populous Metropolitan Areas Tokyo, Japan: 27,242,000 Bombay, India: 15,725,000 Shanghai, China: 13,659,000

Highest Mountains Mount Everest, Tibet-Nepal: 8,848 m (29,028 ft.); K2, Pakistan: 8,611 m (28,250 ft.)

Lowest Point Dead Sea: 408 m (1,339 ft.) below sea level

Longest River Yangzi (China): 6,380 km (3,964 mi.)

Wettest Place Mawsynram, Assam, India: average annual rainfall 11,873 mm (467 in.)

Most Densely Populated Country Singapore: 5,654 people per sq km (14,644 people per sq mi.)

Least Densely Populated Country Mongolia: 1.5 people per sq km (4 people per sq mi.)

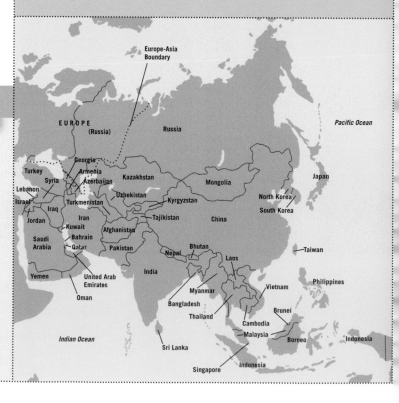

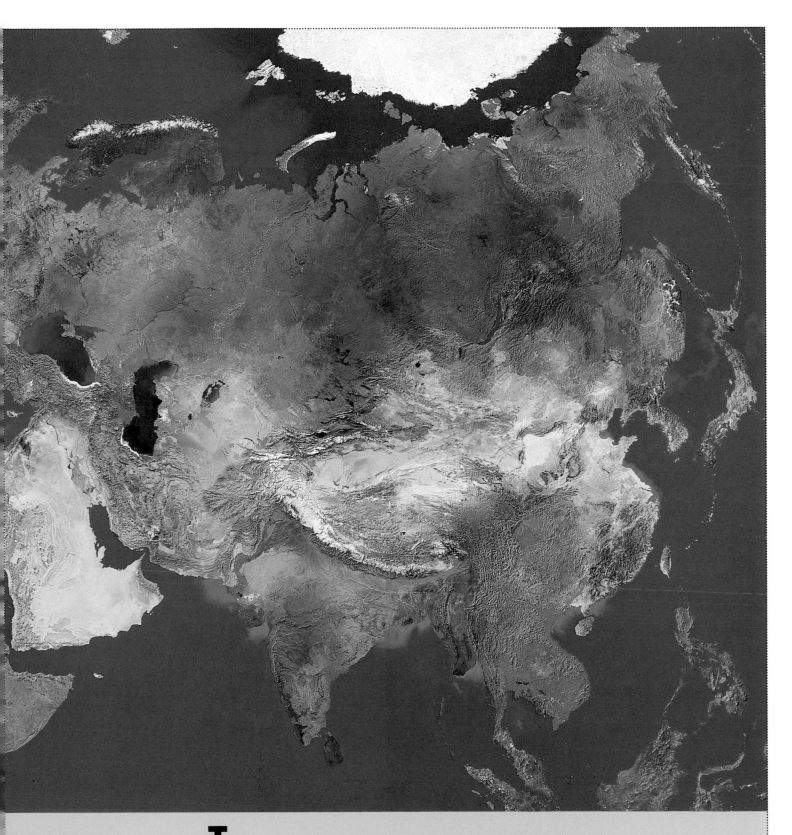

As Seen from Space

The continent of Asia, seen here in a satellite photo, makes up one-third of the landmass of the world. Green areas indicate vegetation: the coniferous forests that cover much of Siberia in northern Asia and the lush tropical forests of Southeast Asia. The barren land of the deserts and the snowcapped mountains of the Himalaya cut a wide swath through the south.

Siberia and Central Asia

Siberia covers 7,511,000 sq km (almost 3 million sq mi.) of Russia. It stretches from the Ural Mountains in the west to mountains along the Bering Sea, and from the Arctic Ocean south to Mongolia. Known for its frigid **climate,** Siberia is home to the coldest inhabited place on earth—Verkhoyansk, where the temperature once plunged to -68°C (-90°F). Dense **coniferous** forests cover much of Siberia, but in the west farmers raise wheat, oats, potatoes, and sun-flowers in fertile soil. Dairy farms also flourish there.

South of the Urals lie the nations of central Asia—Uzbekistan, Turkmenistan, Tajikistan, Kazakhstan, and Kyrgyzstan. Part of the Soviet Union until 1991, these newly independent nations have joined the CIS, the Commonwealth of Independent States, and are now working to develop their own **economy.**

Where in the World?

[Russia]
Russia (Siberia)
Uzbekistan
Kazakhstan
Kyrgyzstan
Turkmenistan
Tajikistan

Milk Pops

Would **You** *Believe?*

In winter sidewalk vendors in Siberia do not sell milk in cartons but in frozen chunks just like big Popsicles *(left).* Customers carry the milk home by the wood handle, then thaw it out to drink it.

A Kyrgyz Storyteller

Eyes closed and hands waving, a storyteller from Kyrgyzstan holds the full attention of his audience inside a **yurt.** In the past in Asia, Arabia, and Africa, storytellers passed on the history of the region to new generations; theirs is still an honored profession for the entertainment of all ages.

Frozen Land

Along the Arctic shore of Siberia, the land is frozen. In the short summers only the top layer of the soil thaws, but below the surface it stays frozen permanently—a condition called **permafrost.** Buried in this ground are a wealth of coal, oil, natural gas, and minerals. Arctic foxes, bears, sables, and snowshoe hares roam the land. The Yakut people of Siberia keep large herds of reindeer *(below)*.

Secrets below the Ice

A group of youngsters is getting together for a spirited game of ice hockey on Siberia's frozen Lake Baikal. This is the largest freshwater lake in the world—and the deepest. At its deepest point the water reaches down to about 1,600 m (1 mi.). Scientists believe Lake Baikal formed about 25 million years ago. They are now in the process of drilling through layers of mud 7 km (4 mi.) thick on the lake's bottom to look for clues about the earth's climate over the past 250,000 years.

The Case of the Disappearing Sea

Once the world's fourth largest lake, the Aral Sea, shared by Uzbekistan and Kazakhstan, has lost two-thirds of its water volume, as shown in blue on the map *(right)*. The **rivers** that feed it have been diverted to irrigate fields nearby, stranding boats on a **desert** shore.

Aral Sea

Uzbekistan

Uzbekistan, a center of Muslim **culture,** has many places of worship called mosques *(below)* and seminaries where students study the Islamic religion.

China and Mongolia

Ancient China

China is only slightly larger than the United States but it has nearly one billion more people. Only 10 percent of the country can be farmed, and most of the landmass is covered with **mountains,** arid **grassland,** or **desert,** so feeding all of China's people is a difficult task. Nearly 90 percent of the people live in the low-lying eastern part of the country, particularly on the fertile banks of the Yangzi and Yellow Rivers. The Yellow River, the muddiest river in the world, picks up nutrient-rich soil called **loess** from the edge of the Gobi Desert and deposits it along its banks, creating fertile soil for farming. But the buildup of **silt** can create problems as well. Massive flooding is common, earning the Yellow River another name—China's Sorrow.

In the cold northeast, coal, oil, iron, and timber fuel thriving **industries.**

Where in the World?

One Baby per Family

Would You Believe?

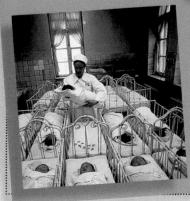

China has the world's largest population—and it grows by 17 million every year. The government has set a limit of one child per family, so almost everyone is an only child—unless you are lucky enough to have a twin.

Modern China

Hong Kong, the island port off the southeast coast of China, is one of the most important trading and banking centers of the world. In 1997, after 155 years of British rule, Hong Kong—and its six million people—was returned to China.

Walls and Palaces

Stretching for at least 2,400 km (1,500 mi.) across northern China, the Great Wall *(left)* was built more than 2,000 years ago to keep out foreign invaders. In the capital, at Beijing's Forbidden City *(above)*, even Chinese citizens could not enter the emperor's 9,999-room complex of ancient palaces.

Mongolia

Southern China

A Sharp Divide

The Yangzi River divides China roughly in half. To the north, the weather is generally cold and droughts are common. Wheat, millet, and sorghum are the main crops. The south, as seen along the dramatic limestone hills in the Guilin region, is warm and wet—perfect for growing rice and fishing.

The boys above are racing their horses across the **steppes,** or flat, treeless grasslands, of Mongolia. They are most likely the sons of **nomads,** people who tend livestock and move from place to place in search of fresh pasture for their sheep, goats, cattle, and horses. In higher elevations, they also raise yaks, shaggy oxlike animals that provide milk, butter, and meat. When on the move, Mongolians live in tent-like **yurts** that can be folded up. Mongolia is situated between Russia and China on a high elevation and along-side the Gobi Desert. Rainfall is minimal in the desert and temperatures are extreme, with hot summers and bitterly cold winters, but underground water is available.

Himalayan Region

The Himalaya are sometimes called "the roof of the world" because the **mountain** ranges that carry that name are the tallest on earth: Their highest peak, Mount Everest, reaches to a soaring 8,848 m (29,028 ft.). The Himalaya extend for about 2,400 km (1,500 mi.) across Asia, forming a dividing line between India and central Asia, and cutting through northern India and the countries of Nepal and Bhutan. Most of the people of Nepal and Bhutan farm and raise livestock in the lower elevations, and tend yak herds on the mountains in summer. This also holds true for Tibet, an **autonomous** region of China that occupies the highest **plateau** on earth—4,880 m (16,000 ft.) above sea level. Mineral resources are abundant there and include gold, iron, and copper, but transportation is difficult—Tibet has few roads and no railroads.

Where in the World?

Tibet   Bhutan

Nepal

What a View!

The Potola Palace, once the residence of the Tibetan leader of Buddhism, called the Dalai Lama, sits on a 120-m (400-ft.)-high hillside above Tibet's capital of Lhasa *(right)*. Briefly independent in the early 20th century, Tibet came under Chinese Communist rule in 1959, and the Dalai Lama, who was also the head of the government, fled to India.

Yak Attack

Sturdy yaks pick their way along a snowy path in the mountains of Nepal, carrying heavy loads. Yaks are well adapted for life at high elevations—they can survive very cold temperatures and thrive on the scarce vegetation. The animals serve where trucks cannot go, hauling goods for trade across the wind-swept plateaus and over the difficult mountain passes.

Living in Thin Air

This Sherpa girl, from the high Himalayan valleys of Nepal, carries a sickle for cutting grass and a basket held in typical fashion on a strap across her forehead. She is used to hard work at high **altitudes.** At elevations above 3,000 m (10,000 ft.) there is less oxygen in the air than at sea level, and the air is said to be thinner. If you're not used to breathing it, you can become short of breath or even dizzy. Sherpas, a Buddhist people originally from Tibet, often carry heavy gear to the peaks for mountain climbers without becoming ill. Scientists believe they may have unique genes that enable them to use oxygen so efficiently.

Life in Bhutan

Most natives of Bhutan, such as the family shown with all their possessions, grow grain and raise livestock for a living. A kingdom tucked between Tibet and India on the eastern slopes of the Himalaya, Bhutan works hard to preserve its **culture:** The women still weave clothing on old-fashioned looms, and the men compete at archery, Bhutan's traditional sport.

Indian Subcontinent

Dust Storm!

The Asian landmass south of the Himalaya is so large that it is called the Indian subcontinent. The nations of India, Pakistan, and Bangladesh make up most of the subcontinent, with Bhutan and Nepal tucked into the northeast corner. When British colonial rule of the region ended in 1947, Pakistan and Bangladesh were established as one nation called East and West Pakistan. Bangladesh declared its independence from this union in 1971. With an area of 3,287,590 sq km (1,269,346 sq mi.) India is by far the largest country in the subcontinent. Its population is nearly one billion, and almost 16 million people live in and near Bombay, the largest city. Although many of its people are poor, India produces enough food for its population and raises a lot of cotton. Roughly 70 percent of India's people are agricultural workers, but the cities boast many modern **industries.**

Where in the World?

Indian women, on their way to fetch water from a well, huddle together as a sudden dust storm blows in. People living in the dry northwestern state of Rajasthan endure many such storms in April and May, the dry months before the wet **monsoon** season.

Tea and Spices in Sri Lanka

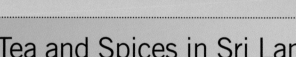

A lush tea plantation covers the hillsides in Sri Lanka *(below)*, an island country off the southeastern coast of India. The country's fertile flatlands and rolling **hills** produce tea, rubber, coconut, cocoa, coffee, tobacco, and spices for export.

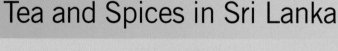

Kashmir

Beneath the majestic peaks of the Himalaya, houseboats float on Nagin Lake in Kashmir. The once independent state of Kashmir is now divided between India and Pakistan. Traditional handicrafts include cashmere: fine woolen cloth woven from the hair of a goat.

India's Marble Wonder

Built in the 17th century to honor the emperor's dead wife, the Taj Mahal, pictured below, took 22,000 workers 22 years to complete.

Pakistan

Bent over their work, these laborers sort baskets of apricots in a **mountain** valley located in Pakistan. Cotton, wheat, rice, and fruits are among the country's commercial crops, with the richest farmland found near the Indus River. Because much of the country is semi-arid land or **desert**, Pakistan has developed an irrigation system that brings water to the land through 58,000 km (36,000 mi.) of canals and 1.6 million field ditches.

Strange But TRUE!

Vanishing Islands

In Bangladesh, land is scarce, so farmers often cultivate **islands** that have been built up from **silt** that washed down the mountains during the monsoon rains. Some of these islands stay in the rivers for 30 years or longer; others may wash away with the next storm, taking the people along.

Japan Korea, and the Philippines

Japan is an **archipelago,** or a group of **islands,** that stretches more than 2,790 km (1,734 mi.) in the Pacific **Ocean.** Of the 4,000 mountainous islands that make up the country, Honshu is the largest and is the heart of modern Japan; 80 percent of the population lives there.

Japan ruled the nearby Korean **peninsula** from 1910 until 1948. Since then, Korea has been divided into two separate and independent countries. To the south of Japan and Korea are Taiwan and the Philippines, an archipelago of 7,100 islands. These tropical islands are, like Japan, susceptible to earthquakes, typhoons, and volcanic eruptions.

Japan and Taiwan have become wealthy from manufacturing, and North and South Korea employ many people in **industry,** but the people who live in the Philippines depend on agriculture, fishing, and forestry for their livelihood.

Where in the World?

North Korea

Japan

South Korea

Taiwan

Philippines

No cookies and milk for these Japanese schoolchildren—they munch on rice cakes, a favorite treat. Rice, the basic food of the Japanese, is grown on more than half the farmland in Japan.

Korea

The pond at Kyongbokkung Palace is a peaceful oasis in Seoul, South Korea's bustling capital of nearly 12 million. South Korea occupies nearly half of the 1,000-km (600-mi.)-long Korean peninsula. The other half is governed by Communist North Korea. Both countries have large tracts of farmland, but more people work in modern industries.

Philippines

Like Japan, the Philippines are an archipelago. Only about 700 of the 7,100 Philippine Islands are inhabited. **Mountains** take up much of the land, so farmers terrace the lower slopes to grow rice *(left)* or cultivate the fertile **plains** along the coast. The tropical islands' most important crops include rice, corn, sugarcane, coconuts, bananas, tobacco, coffee, and pineapples.

Gateway to Japan

Rising out of the sea, this graceful Japanese gate, or torii, marks the entrance to the sacred Itsukushima shrine on Miyajima, an island near Hiroshima. Shrines like this one welcome the spirits of the water to the island country. Shinto, Japan's native religion, honors the spirits found in nature, and torii are often placed at the entrances to temples.

Bright Lights of Tokyo

A jumble of colorful lights mark the shopping district of Tokyo, the capital city of Japan. One of the world's most important financial and communications centers, Tokyo and the surrounding area are best known for the manufacture of electronic equipment, automobiles, cameras, and other products. These goods are shipped all over the world from the city's harbor on Tokyo Bay or from the nearby seaport of Yokohama. Founded in the 12th century and almost completely destroyed by an earthquake and fire in 1923, Tokyo is now one of the most modern cities in the world.

Would You Believe?

Hotel Capsules

Seen through doors that look like big TV screens, guests rest in capsules that are rented out like hotel rooms in Tokyo. In this crowded city, space is expensive, and some people make do with this kind of box, equipped with everything they need for an overnight stay.

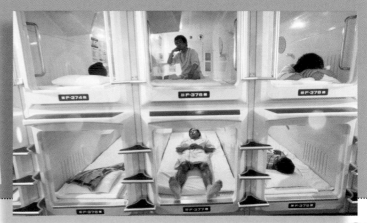

Southeast Asia

Two boys cross a bridge that is suspended over a shallow valley in Malaysia's rain forest. The region has a great variety of plant life.

Many different nations and **cultures** reside in the lush, tropical region that is Southeast Asia. On the mainland to the west is Myanmar, the country formerly called Burma. To its east lie Thailand, Laos, Cambodia, and Vietnam, where fishing is a major **industry.** Thailand's territory wends south into the long Malay Peninsula; the nation of Malaysia occupies the lower part of the peninsula (another part of Malaysia lies on the **island** of Borneo). Off the peninsula's southern tip is the island of Singapore, home to one of Asia's most important seaports. Farther east more than 13,000 islands make up the nation of Indonesia, which produces more rice per person than either China or India does. Southeast Asia is hit every year by fierce **monsoon** winds and driving rains, which bring life to the fields and to the **rain forests.**

Where in the World?

Laos · Vietnam
Myanmar
Thailand
Cambodia · Brunei
Malaysia
Singapore · Indonesia · Indonesia
Indonesia

A Gift of Food

In an alley in Rangoon, Myanmar, Buddhist monks carry bowls of food given to them for their breakfast by other faithful Buddhists. Monks not only vow to give up all personal possessions, they even depend on others to feed them. When the family in the foreground finishes eating, they will sell meals to passersby.

Thailand's Floating Supermarket

Farmers wearing broad straw hats sell vegetables and fruits from their boats in a canal near Bangkok, the capital of Thailand. Their eager customers line the shore. Even though Thailand has modern roads, many people still use old canals for travel and to bring food to market.

Winds of Change

Let's Compare

During Monsoon

Monsoon winds and heavy rains have caused the Mekong River in Cambodia to rise, nearly flooding this house.

After Monsoon

When the floodwaters recede, or get lower, lush vegetation grows in the fertile earth left behind.

A Tractor with Horns

This Indonesian girl is riding a water buffalo, which farmers use to pull heavy loads and plow the fields. Ten percent of the land can be farmed; most is devoted to rice. More than 200 million people inhabit the **archipelago** of some 13,000 mountainous islands that make up Indonesia.

Middle East

Europeans coined the term Middle East to describe the vast region from India west to Egypt, the geographic crossroads between Europe and the Far East. The Middle East includes Afghanistan, Iran, Iraq, Jordan, Syria, Egypt, Israel, Lebanon, and Turkey, as well as Georgia, Armenia, and Azerbaijan, and the island of Cyprus. The region also takes in the seven nations of the Arabian **Peninsula** —Saudi Arabia, Yemen, Oman, the United Arab Emirates, Qatar, Bahrain, and Kuwait. Bordered by the Red Sea, the Persian Gulf, and the Arabian Sea, the area holds the world's largest oil reserves. Most people in the Middle East are Muslims and share Islamic **culture** amid many different languages and national customs. All come together during the annual hajj, when thousands of faithful make the pilgrimage to Mecca in Saudi Arabia.

Where in the World?

Oil beneath the Inland Sea

The Caspian Sea was once famous only for caviar but is now dotted with oil rigs, holding oil deposits as large as those in the United States. The sea borders Azerbaijan and Iran and is the largest lake in the world—larger than all of America's Great Lakes together.

Life on the Move

The veiled Bedouin women at left tend children in a tent divided by carpets into separate living quarters for men and women. The Bedouin of the Arabian Peninsula, as well as many other Muslims, stick to strict religious laws that prescribe dress and behavior. The Bedouin are **nomads,** wandering from place to place to herd their sheep and camels. Food is scarce in this desert land, so most Bedouin exist primarily on a diet of camel's milk, rice, and dates.

Syrian Ruins

Ruins of the ancient city of Palmyra in Syria stand as reminders of past glory on the caravan trade route.

Crossroads of Two Continents

Istanbul, Turkey, is the only city in the world to straddle two continents. Part lies in Europe (foreground), the rest in Asia across the Strait of Bosporus.

Houses in Rock Towers

About 1,600 years ago, people in Cappadocia, in central Turkey, began digging into towering spires of soft rock to carve out homes and churches. Many are still lived in today near the village of Urgup.

Afghanistan

Shoppers at narrow market stalls on a town square in Herat, Afghanistan, are framed by ancient mud-brick walls. The city in the northwestern **mountains** along the Hari Rud River endures after many wars of conquest. One of the first conquerors was Alexander the Great in the fourth century BC.

Hello?

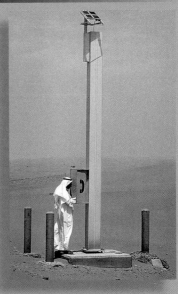

Stranded on a bleak desert track of Saudi Arabia, a driver uses a solar-powered radio-telephone to call for help.

Africa The Giant

Africa, the second largest **continent,** spreads across more than one-fifth of the earth's land surface. It includes the largest hot **desert** in the world, the longest **river,** a wide band of tropical **rain forest,** volcanoes, and many of the world's most unusual animals and plants. Africa's landscape has changed little in 500 million years. It is the oldest stable landmass in the world. The earliest human remains on earth—more than three million years old—are found in Africa, though today's human population there is smaller than that of India. More than 50 countries share the continent, their peoples speaking hundreds of different languages. Famous early civilizations flourished in Egypt (3000 BC), Ghana (AD 500), Zimbabwe (AD 1000), and Songhay—modern-day Mali and Niger (AD 1400). European powers ruled much of Africa throughout the 19th century, adding settlers and their customs to Africa's rich mix. The vibrant, diverse **cultures** that have developed in Africa reflect the importance of its **natural resources,** including gold and diamonds, on the trade routes of the world since ancient times.

The Tropical Savanna

Vast areas of Africa look like the plains of the Masai Mara Reserve in Kenya *(above).* This natural grassland, called savanna, or veld in South Africa, is home to a wide variety of animals, including elephants, wildebeests, zebras, giraffes, hyenas, and lions. The animals are able to share the food sources because they specialize. Giraffes prefer the leaves of acacia trees, zebras eat grasses, elephants like leaves and shrubs, and the carnivores kill and scavenge meat. The Masai people hunt, herd animals, and gather wild food on the plains in order to add to their milk-based diet.

Fast FACTS

Land Area 30,065,000 sq km (11,609,000 sq mi.)

Population 654,600,000

Largest Desert Sahara: 9,065,000 sq km (3,500,000 sq mi.). This is as big as the continental United States!

Highest Mountain Mount Kilimanjaro (Tanzania): 5,895 m (19,340 ft.)

Longest River Nile (Egypt): 6,825 km (4,241 mi.)

Largest Island Madagascar: 587,000 sq km (226,658 sq mi.). It is the fourth largest island in the world.

Largest Cities Lagos, Nigeria: 10,878,000; Cairo, Egypt: 9,900,000

World's Hottest Place Dalol, Ethiopia, has an average annual temperature of 34°C (93°F).

Lowest Point Lake Assal (Djibouti): 156 m (512 ft.) below sea level

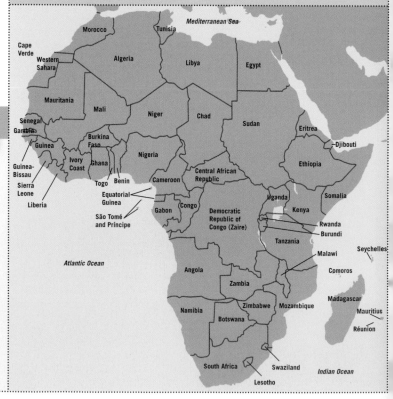

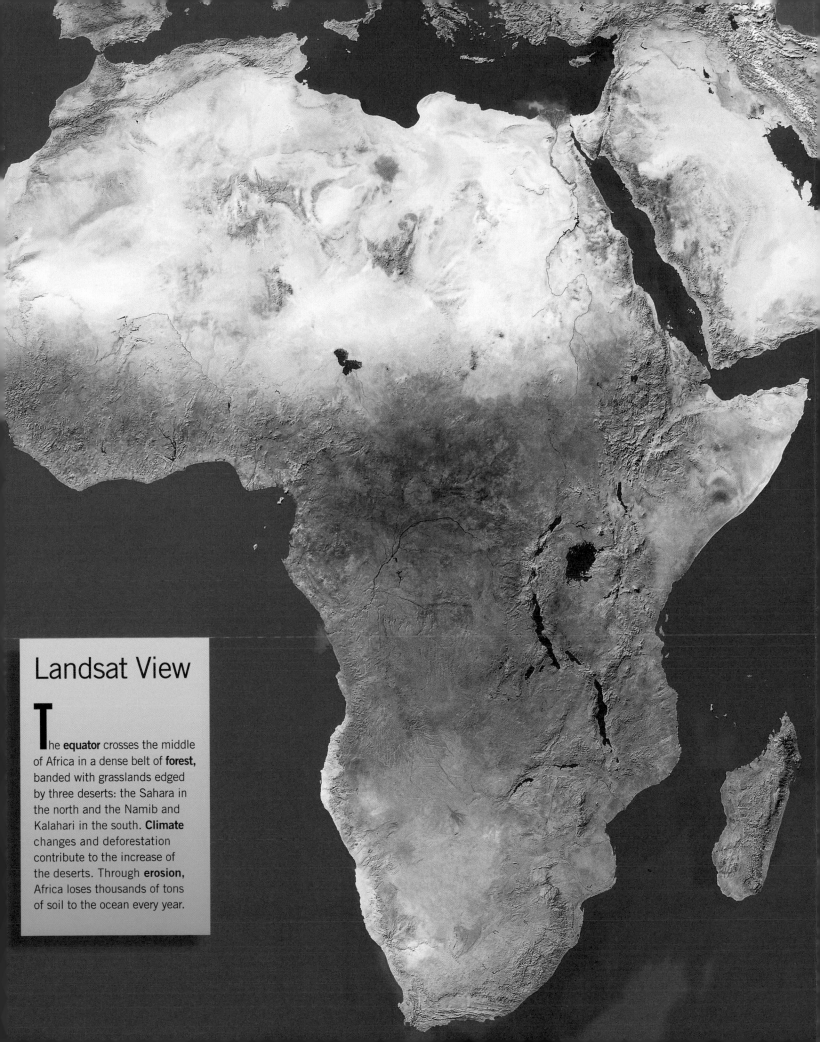

Landsat View

The **equator** crosses the middle of Africa in a dense belt of **forest,** banded with grasslands edged by three deserts: the Sahara in the north and the Namib and Kalahari in the south. **Climate** changes and deforestation contribute to the increase of the deserts. Through **erosion,** Africa loses thousands of tons of soil to the ocean every year.

North Africa

A land cradled between three seas—the Atlantic **Ocean,** the Mediterranean Sea, and the Red Sea—and the great Sahara, North Africa is blessed with some prosperity. Oil and gas wells in Libya and Algeria, plus a vibrant trade with other Mediterranean nations, provide a stable livelihood for many of its people. Though most of the land is dry, hot **desert,** snow may block the high passes of the Atlas Mountains on the northwest rim of the area. The mighty Nile River in the east fostered the ancient civilizations of Egypt and Nubia (modern Sudan). When camels were introduced into Africa more than 2,000 years ago, caravans forged trade routes across the Sahara to exchange goods from Europe and Asia for gold and salt mined in West and central Africa. In AD 640 Muslim peoples from Arabia invaded North Africa; today more **ethnic** Arabs live in Africa than in Saudi Arabia.

Where in the World?

The Sahara

Rally cars speed through the Sahara at the midpoint of the 17-day Paris-Dakar race. The Arabic name for Sahara means "brown and empty," although 10,000 years ago the land was green and got plenty of rain. A drying cycle is now increasing desert acreage, especially in the southern area called the Sahel.

On the Nile

Sailboats called feluccas still navigate on the Nile, in Egypt, as they have for centuries. The tradition began in ancient times, when few roads joined the cities: People traveled on the river or walked along its banks. As far as the river's water can irrigate the land, farmers grow wheat, vegetables, and date palms; beyond the river's influence, the land is desert.

Mountain Strongholds

In a village tucked into a fold of Morocco's Atlas Mountains, people make the most of every strip of land to grow crops. In this dry land the mark of wealth is owning a garden. The long, winding road is lined with almond trees, and the fields alongside are carefully irrigated with water from village wells. Farmers in sheltered valleys like this one cultivate wheat and other grain and keep small herds of goats, sheep, or cattle. Their houses are built of stone and mortar. These types of settlements were built like fortresses of old: Protected by the mountains on one side, they were positioned high enough for inhabitants to see raiding desert enemies in time to organize defenses.

In Morocco's south, farmers grow tomatoes, olives, grapes, and citrus fruit, and along the oases they grow date palms.

World Trade Center

The market, or suk, at right, held under arches built in the Arab style in Tunis, Tunisia, displays the crosscurrents of culture in North Africa. Shoppers wearing traditional Islamic and Western clothing mingle among merchants who sell local farm produce, imported foodstuffs from Asia and Europe, housewares, native pottery, embossed leatherwork, and electronics.

People   The Tuareg

This Tuareg boy with his decorated sword upholds a heritage of nomadic herders and fierce rebels against Arab and European invaders. Grazing their camels and goats over vast areas, the Tuareg measure economic worth in numbers of animals. Their caravans trade in salt and potash across the Sahara. Blue robes and veils protect them from the desert sand.

West Africa

Desert, seacoast, tropical **forest,** wide **grassland,** and busy urban centers all exist within West Africa. The fabled city of Timbuktu in Mali was an important destination for caravans that carried salt and gold across the Sahara and became a seat of Islamic learning in the 1400s. The great empires of Songhay (in Mali) and Ashanti (in Ghana) flourished under local rulers until 1900. Then European traders came to West Africa for gold, metals, timber, and slaves; by 1914 Europe governed all of West Africa except Liberia, a country founded by African Americans who had returned to Africa. Independent again today, West African nations have political boundaries set by the Europeans, sometimes crossing **ethnic** lines and uniting peoples with very diverse customs. Strong ties to Europe through trade and **culture** remain.

Where in the World?

Cape Verde
Mauritania
Senegal
Gambia
Guinea-Bissau
Guinea
Sierra Leone
Liberia
Ivory Coast
Mali
Burkina Faso
Niger
Nigeria
Chad
Benin
Togo
Ghana
Cameroon
São Tomé and Príncipe

The Marketplace

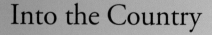

This lively outdoor market in a town in Côte D'Ivoire brings together the culture of three **continents.** People barter for fresh foods, European canned goods, and clothing from Africa and America. Everyone brings a container from home to carry the purchases.

Playing Mancala

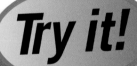
Try it!

Africans enjoy many versions of the game *mancala.* Here 48 pebbles or beans are used as playing pieces. The object is to collect the most in your home bin. Players move in turn. Take all pieces from a bin on your side and drop one in each bin, moving to the right around the board. If you end in your "home," go again.

Skip your opponent's "home." If you end in an empty bin, take the pieces opposite. When one player has all empty bins, the other gets the rest of the pieces to end the game. The person with the most pieces in the home bin wins.

Home Bin

Home Bin

Into the Country

Women in Gambia till a field with hoes. The dense jungle behind them, nourished by the Gambia River, forms a rich expanse of evergreen forest where monkeys, birds, ant-eaters, pygmy hippopotamuses, and snakes live. People grow beans, peanuts, cocoa, cassava (an edible root), millet and sorghum (grains), rice, and cotton in the fields.

At Home in Mali

Husband, two wives, and six children make up the Natomo family, shown above on the roof of their house in Kouakourou, Mali. Among the possessions they prize are cooking pots, a bicycle, a transistor radio, and an adobe brick mold. Mosquito netting covers the outdoor bed, where sleepers can cool off at night.

Storytellers

Many African people enjoy storytelling—not just the children, but the adults as well. The tales explain the natural world and its inter-connections, recount the history, dictate customs and morals within villages and ethnic groups, and, of course, amuse everyone. In many villages "Storyteller" is an official job, and people aspire to be known as the best one in the region.

Magnificent Mud

This mosque in Jenné, Mali, stands on the site of a Muslim house of prayer of the 1300s. Its mud walls plastered onto a timber frame must be repaired each year after the rains.

East Africa

E ast Africa is known for scenes that seem "typically African," including **savannas** with grazing wild-life and people in colorful costumes. It is also the home of extremes, including Africa's highest **mountains** and biggest lake, and unstable geology, with the edges of **tectonic plates** slowly splitting the **continent** apart and perhaps one day opening to the sea. Drought and war have afflicted parts of East Africa since the 1970s, forcing many people to leave their homelands. Food shortages and growing populations have also caused problems in this delicately balanced landscape. Though humans and animals have lived here together for more than three million years, people and animals now get in each other's way. National game preserves in Kenya and Tanzania have been successful in protecting wild animals and encouraging both Africans and foreign visitors to appreciate them.

Where in the World?

The Masai

T hese Masai girls wear traditional clothing in a village in Kenya. Their beaded collars and ornaments indicate whether they are married or available for marriage offers. The Masai are famous warriors and cattle herders living in Kenya and Tanzania. Mainly vegetarian, the Masai also drink the milk and blood of living cattle to add protein to their diet.

Let's Compare

Modern City

Nairobi, Kenya, sports skyscrapers and a city atmosphere greatly influenced by European building styles. But the many parks around town include areas where cheetahs and elephants roam.

Modern Village

Round houses are still the preferred style in many African villages. The walls are made of woven wood covered with mud; roofs are thatched with reeds and grass. These houses are very practical, cheap to build and easy to repair with local materials.

The Oldest Footprints

A researcher checks footprints that were made 3.6 million years ago, when three people walked on a muddy path near Laetoli, Tanzania. Volcanic ash drifting down from simmering eruptions nearby covered the tracks and preserved them. Archaeologist Mary Leakey led the 1976 expedition that discovered the prints, which are the earliest record of humans walking upright.

The Savanna

Though it stands quite close to the **equator,** Mount Kilimanjaro shrouds its icy 5,895-m (19,340-ft.) peak in snow all year long. Zebra and antelope herds in Amboseli National Park, Kenya, below the mountain promote healthy grass mixtures by browsing on different grass species.

The Great Rift Valley

Africa is showing the strain where separating tectonic plates form an 80-km (50-mi.)-wide split running north and south through East Africa. Volcanoes, fault lines, hot springs, and lakes filled with harsh sulfur compounds are signs of geologic change in progress. Flocks of flamingos nest at the lakes, feeding on algae that thrive in the warm water.

Great Rift Valley

Central Africa

Warm tropical **rain forest** covers much of central Africa, where the Congo **River** drains from the highlands of the countries of Congo and the Democratic Republic of Congo into the Atlantic Ocean. Unusual animals flourish here: an air-breathing fish, the world's largest beetle, pygmy chimpanzees, thumbless monkeys, venomous vipers, and giant antelopes. The **climate** is good for farming: Families cut clearings in the rain forest, burn the timber, and grow cassava, bananas, and corn. When the soil loses its fertility, farmers move on to clear new land, and the **forest** grows back. This part of the continent is rich in **natural resources** such as oil, gas, and metals. Once ruled by Belgium, Portugal, Spain, and France, central African countries have been independent since the 1960s, but civil wars have plagued the area. Today there is renewed hope for peace and democratic government.

Where in the World?

Central African Republic

Equatorial Guinea

Gabon

Democratic Republic of Congo (Zaire)

Congo

Angola

Zambia

Banana trees *(bottom left)* reach to the edge of a village in the Democratic Republic of Congo, planted where the rain forest has been cleared. Africans grow about 60 different **cultivars** of bananas, some for eating fresh, some for cooking. Bananas form the **staple** diet in areas where they grow all year round.

Giant Plants!

A woman with a child on her back strides through the lush forest of the Ruwenzori Mountains between Uganda and the Democratic Republic of Congo. At **altitudes** above 3,600 m (12,000 ft.) giant species of familiar plants flourish. Lobelias—looking like bottle brushes—and groundsel—with green mop heads—may reach 9 m (30 ft.) high.

The Congo Basin

In the Democratic Republic of Congo, a fisherman poises his trap over white water to let fish drift into the wide end. Besides the Congo, the river systems of the central African states include the mighty Victoria Falls on the Zambezi in Zimbabwe, Boyoma Falls in Zambia, and Lake Tanganyika.

Dancing for Joy

In Uganda

Outside a village in the Uganda highlands, a man crowned with colobus monkey plumes performs an exuberant dance. Dance is more than entertainment here: It is a ritual that connects the spirit world with the everyday world.

Who Are the Forest People?

About 165,000 Forest People, known for their small stature—they are less than 1.5 m (5 ft.) tall—live in central Africa. They hunt and gather food in the wild and make camp dwellings of leaves covering a frame of branches. The Forest People move often so game and resources are not stressed. Renowned for their expertise in herbal medicines, they believe the forest is a living being and protect it lovingly.

Southern Africa

The heart of southern Africa is a sloping **plateau** of **grassland,** bounded by a 3,300-m (11,000-ft.)-high mountainous rim above the coasts of the Atlantic and Indian Oceans. The region includes the Namib Desert in Namibia, boasting the world's highest sand dunes, the world's largest inland **delta** at the **mouth** of the Okavango River in Botswana, and even the world's largest man-made excavation—the now abandoned Big Hole at the Kimberley diamond mines in South Africa. The nation of South Africa, with many of its citizens descended from Dutch and English settlers, dominated its neighbors for most of the 20th century. Independent today, these smaller countries are developing their agricultural bases and mineral resources, some still controlled by foreign owners. About 300 kinds of native mammals, including fur seals, and 400 species of reptiles share the land.

Where in the World?

Mozambique
Zimbabwe
Madagascar
Namibia Botswana
Swaziland
South
Africa
Lesotho

Farming the Land

A range of **climates,** soils, and traditions allows South Africans variety in farm produce, as seen in the green landscape above. Terracing preserves soil on the slopes, but the shelter belt of trees, which is an ancient European farming practice, works here too, taming wind that blows soil and damages tender crops. Farmers grow corn, wheat, sugarcane, citrus fruit, peanuts, tobacco, millet, and sorghum or they raise cattle.

Madagascar

It lies only 400 km (250 mi.) from Africa in the Indian Ocean, but this **island** was first settled by seafaring Indonesians. Lemurs, the world's biggest chameleon, and some 300 species of butterfly struggle to survive as human need for farmland threatens **habitats.** Conservation programs hope to curb soil **erosion,** which stains miles of ocean red after heavy rains.

In the Bush

This San hunter in Botswana's Kalahari trusts his hunting and gathering skills with traditional spear and arrows. To cover the miles, he uses modern transportation.

Cape of Good Hope

European-style houses nestle in the curve of the bay at Cape Town, South Africa, with the Cape of Good Hope looming behind. Named by sailors pursuing the old trade route to the Indies, the Cape's harbor protected their ships from violent storms off the tip of Africa.

Tutu and Mandela

Under the apartheid system from 1948 to 1991, black South Africans could not vote and had few rights. Nelson Mandela *(right),* a lawyer imprisoned for 28 years, helped draft a nonracial constitution, received the Nobel Peace Prize, and was president of South Africa from 1994 to 1999. Retired archbishop Desmond Tutu, a Nobel laureate in 1984, set up the Truth and Reconciliation Commission to hear and judge apartheid crimes.

Botswana's Okavango Delta

Small boats are the best way to travel through this country where the narrow channels of the Okavango River wind through thickets of grasses and reeds. Hippos, crocodiles, lions, cheetahs, herons, wildebeests, and swamp antelopes make their home here. The Botswana government encourages photo safaris in the delta.

Underground Riches

A miner drills the rockface at the Einer gold mine in South Africa. Besides gold, South African countries mine precious diamonds, iron, uranium, and copper. The giant Cullinan Diamond, weighing 560 g (1.25 lb.), came from South Africa. Many mines are far away from settlements, so workers live apart from their families.

Australia New Zealand, & Oceania

Australia is the only country that consists of an entire **continent;** it has no borders with any other nation. Australia is about the size of the United States, not including Alaska and Hawaii. It is the smallest of earth's seven continents, but the sixth largest country in the world. The name comes from the Latin word *australis,* which means "southern." Because Australia lies south of—or "down under"—the **equator,** the seasons are reversed from those north of the equator. New Year's Day, for example, is celebrated during the summer.

Australia is divided into six states—including the island of Tasmania—and two territories, the Australian Capital Territory and the Northern Territory. All of Australia's major cities—except the capital, Canberra—are located along the coast. Except for Antarctica, Australia is the least densely populated continent because few people (mostly sheep farmers and prospectors) live in the hot interior, known as the Outback.

To the southeast of Australia lies New Zealand, composed of two large **islands** and several smaller ones. The country is situated in a cool, **temperate** zone, where some **grasslands** and exotic **forests** cover the land.

In a half-circle to the north and east of Australia lies Oceania, divided into the island groups of Melanesia, Micronesia, and Polynesia.

The Pinnacles Desert

Among Australia's many dry regions, the Pinnacles in western Australia is unique. This area once had a much wetter **climate** and was covered by forest. Water seeped below the surface where tree roots broke through the firm soil. Chemicals in the water bonded with the sand to form hard columns of rock. Then the climate turned drier, the forest died, and the land became **desert.** Over thousands of years, wind **eroded** the surface soil and exposed these sandstone pillars.

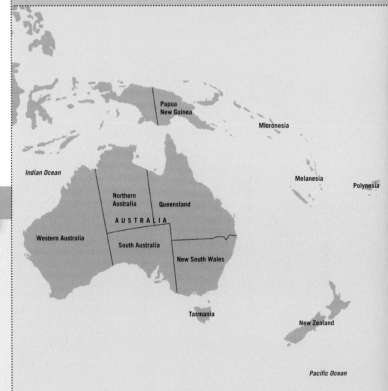

Fast FACTS

Area Australia: 7,682,300 sq km (2,966,153 sq mi.); New Zealand: 269,057 sq km (103,883 sq mi.); Oceania: 583,760 sq km (225,391 sq mi.)

Population Australia: 18,700,000; New Zealand: 3,800,000; Oceania: 7,000,000

Population Density Australia: 2.3 people per sq km (6 per sq mi.); New Zealand: 12.7 per sq km

(33 per sq mi.); Oceania: 3.1 per sq km (8.1 per sq mi.)

Capitals Australia: Canberra; New Zealand: Wellington

Largest Cities (Australia) Sydney: 3,600,000; Melbourne: 3,100,000; Brisbane: 1,300,000

Longest River Darling (Australia): 2,739 km (1,702 mi.)

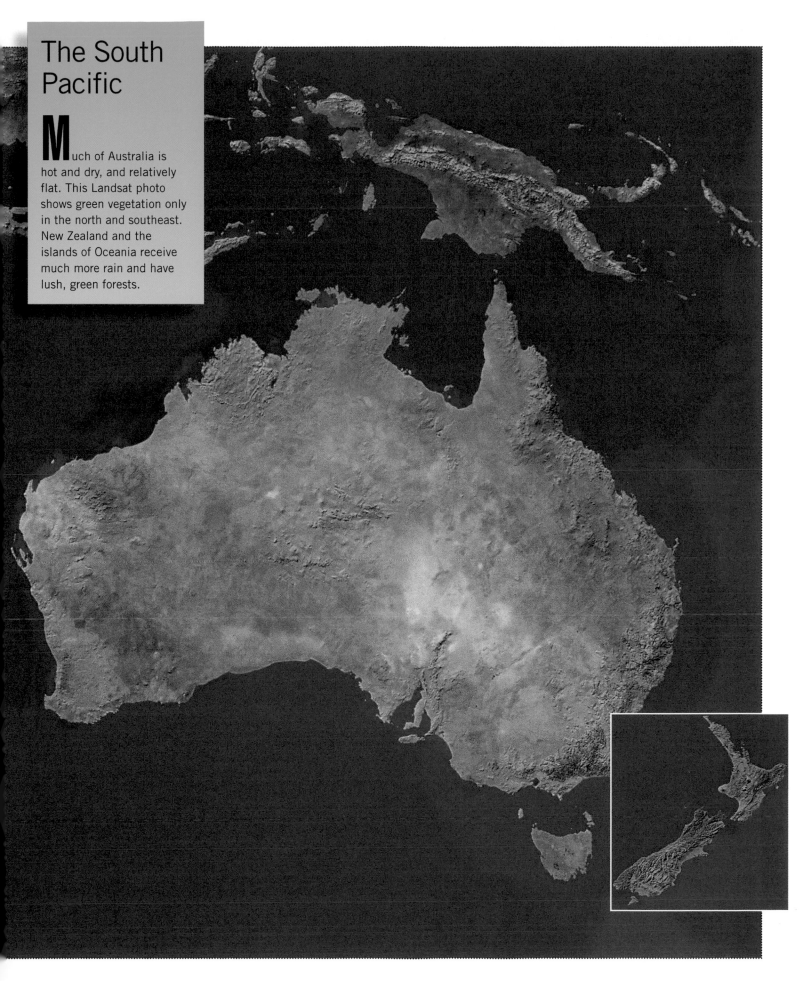

The South Pacific

Much of Australia is hot and dry, and relatively flat. This Landsat photo shows green vegetation only in the north and southeast. New Zealand and the islands of Oceania receive much more rain and have lush, green forests.

Australia and New Zealand

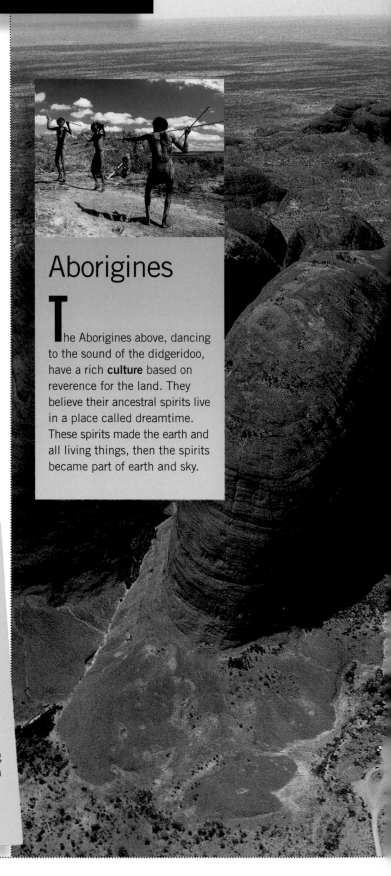

The population of Australia and New Zealand is largely made up of immigrants from Europe. But both of the countries have native peoples. Australia's original inhabitants, called Aborigines, arrived about 50,000 years ago. New Zealand was first settled by the Maori, who sailed there in canoes about seven centuries ago from other **islands** in the South Pacific.

Dutch explorers in the 17th century were the first Europeans to see Australia. After sailing along the north, west, and south coasts, they decided that the land was too dry and barren to be colonized. In 1770, the English captain James Cook explored both New Zealand and Australia's much more inviting east coast and claimed both lands for Great Britain.

Australia was first used by the British as a penal colony—that is, prisoners were sent to live there in exile. Later, both Australia and New Zealand attracted thousands of willing settlers, coming mostly from Great Britain and Ireland.

Aborigines

The Aborigines above, dancing to the sound of the didgeridoo, have a rich **culture** based on reverence for the land. They believe their ancestral spirits live in a place called dreamtime. These spirits made the earth and all living things, then the spirits became part of earth and sky.

Unusual Wildlife

Marsupials, such as the kangaroo at left, are mammals that carry their young in a pouch. Because Australia is a long distance from any other **continent** and its animals evolved in isolation, a wide variety of marsupials thrive there, including koalas, wombats, and Tasmanian devils. Other odd creatures are flightless emus and poison-spurred platypuses.

For thousands of years, this spectacular formation, called Ayers Rock or Uluru, in central Australia has been honored by Aborigines as a holy site, a reminder of the dreamtime spirits who created the earth.

Sydney

With a skyline marked by tall office buildings and the world-famous Opera House *(above, left)*, Sydney is the largest and oldest city in Australia.

Would **You** Believe?

Skiing in Australia

Most people don't think of skiing in Australia's warm **climate,** but it's possible on the peaks of the 2,000-m (6,500-ft.)-high Eastern Highlands.

The Great Barrier Reef

The Great Barrier Reef extends for almost 2,000 km (1,200 mi.) along Australia's northeast coast. It is the largest structure in the world made by living creatures, in this case tiny animals called coral.

New Zealand

New Zealand lies about 1,600 km (1,000 mi.) southeast of Australia. The country's human population of about 3.8 million is outnumbered more than 2 to 1 by cattle and 15 to 1 by sheep!

Both the capital, Wellington (population 327,000), and the largest city, Auckland (population 910,000), are located on North Island. This large island has many **geysers** and hot springs. South Island is rural and boasts spectacular scenery, including a **mountain** range called the Southern Alps with 17 peaks more than 3,000 m (10,000 ft.) high. In the southwest, glaciers have carved deep **fjords** *(below)* that resemble the coastline of Norway. Among the unusual native birds are kiwis, lorikeets, and albatrosses.

Oceania is not a **continent.** The name is used to describe a large region of the Pacific **Ocean** that lies close to, or just south of, the **equator.** Within this area are thousands of **islands.** Most are small in size, made up of coral deposits and fringed with sandy beaches and palm trees. A few are larger, volcanic islands with high, steep **mountain** slopes, covered in dense jungle vegetation. The entire region lies within the Tropics, so the **climate** is hot and, for the most part, humid.

Some **geographers** include Australia and New Zealand in Oceania. But usually it is divided into the regions Melanesia, Micronesia, and Polynesia to reflect the differences in culture and ethnicity of the people. Like Australia and New Zealand, Oceania was explored centuries ago by European seafarers, who claimed the island groups for their homelands. Since the end of World War II, these islands have gradually gained their independence from the former colonial powers.

Would You Believe?

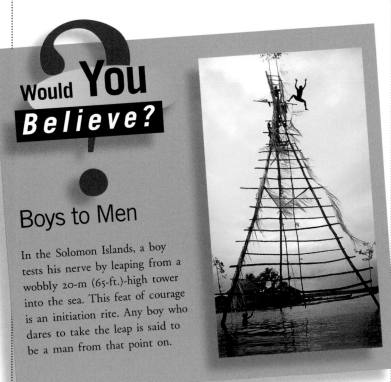

Boys to Men

In the Solomon Islands, a boy tests his nerve by leaping from a wobbly 20-m (65-ft.)-high tower into the sea. This feat of courage is an initiation rite. Any boy who dares to take the leap is said to be a man from that point on.

Palau

Micronesia, a word meaning "tiny islands," consists of about 2,000 islands in the western Pacific. These islands are divided into seven groups, or chains, and all of them at one time were owned by Spain, Germany, Japan, Great Britain, or the United States.

Most of the Micronesian islands, like Palau—shown in the photo above—are small, low-lying coral reefs that form along the crests of submerged mountains that jut up from the floor of the Pacific Ocean. Many are **atolls,** a special kind of coral island that formed around the cone of a sinking volcano. As a result, atolls are roughly circular in shape, with the reefs enclosing a sheltered central lagoon.

Melanesia

Melanesia means "black islands," a name Europeans gave the region after meeting its dark-skinned residents. The region stretches from Fiji, more than 3,000 km (1,800 mi.) east of Australia, to Papua New Guinea, off the continent's northern tip.

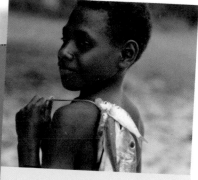

Vanuatu

A boy who lives on Tanna, Vanuatu, proudly shows off his catch. In this chain of Melanesian islands the young fishermen dive after their prey, using a spear to spike the fish.

Polynesia

A Mountain Erupts

Within the huge area of the South Pacific covered by Polynesia and Melanesia are several regions of intense volcanic activity, including New Zealand's North Island, Tonga, and Lopevi and Tanna. The photo below shows the Vasur volcano in full eruption, spewing molten lava into the night sky.

South Seas

Six men row a canoe off the coast of Mooréa in Polynesia. Polynesia, whose name means "many islands," is spread over a vast area of the South Pacific. It contains a mix of smaller coral islands and larger volcanic ones, such as Mooréa.

Antarctica
South End of the World

Antarctica is the only **continent** that does not have a permanent population of humans. Research scientists living for short periods in specially built stations that protect them from the intense cold are Antarctica's only inhabitants. In fact, the extremely frigid **climate** makes the land unfit for most life forms.

Almost twice the size of Australia, Antarctica is the world's largest **desert.** Although we normally associate deserts with hot, dry places, actually the word simply means an arid, barren land. About 98 percent of the continent is covered with a huge sheet of ice that, in some parts, is more than 4 km (2.5 mi.) deep. The few places where the land is clear of snow and ice are almost as lifeless as the surface of the moon. The seas surrounding Antarctica, however, teem with fish and plankton, drawing large numbers of whales, seals, and penguins to the coastal waters.

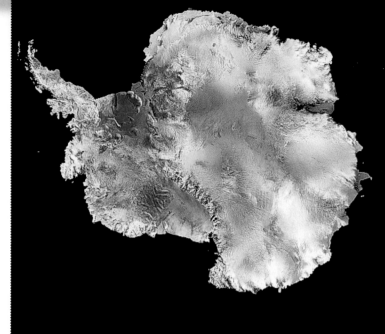

View from Space

This satellite photo shows that Antarctica is almost entirely covered by ice and snow, with only a few **mountain** peaks—and no vegetation at all—visible through the blanket of white.

+ South Pole

Amundsen at the South Pole

Famous **1**
FIRSTS

Roald Amundsen, a Norwegian explorer, led the first expedition to reach the South Pole. He brought sled dogs with him to pull supply sleds while he and his men used cross-country skis.

Fast FACTS

Area 13,209,000 sq km (5,100,400 sq mi.)

Percentage of Land Covered by Ice 98 percent

Highest Mountain Vinson Massif: 5,140 m (16,859 ft.)

Highest Active Volcano Mount Erebus: 3,846 m (12,500 ft.)

Average Annual Snowfall 12 cm (5 in.)

Average Temperature
Summer: -57°C (-70°F)
Winter: -90°C (-130°F)

Thickness of Ice Sheet at the South Pole 2,800 m (9,100 ft.)

First Visit by Humans 1821

First Expedition to Reach South Pole 1911 (Roald Amundsen)

First Flight over South Pole 1929 (Richard E. Byrd)

Well-known symbol of Antarctica, penguins are birds that cannot fly. They walk awkwardly on land, but in the water, their streamlined body, oily feathers, and paddlelike wings make them such excellent swimmers, they are said to fly through the water.

Greenery

There are very few species of plants that can survive the continent's harsh climate. Mosses, **lichens,** and one variety of grass are the largest plants found in Antarctica.

I Was There!

A boy chases chinstrap penguins on King George Island, Antarctica. A few families live for a year or two at the Chilean research station on this northern tip of the continent. One of the boys reported:

"I like summer best because . . . we don't have to wear so much to go outside—only parkas, hats, waterproof boots, and windproof pants."

Barren Valley

Where on EARTH?

In some areas of Antarctica there are valleys that get no snow or ice. High mountains on either side of the valleys keep out the ice sheet, and howling winds evaporate any snow that falls before it reaches the ground. Scientists say that no **precipitation** has touched these valleys for more than two million years!

The World of Economics

Throughout most of human history, land and location have determined how people make their living. In early history, climate and the underlying minerals in rock influenced which plants grew, what animals fed on them, and whether human hunter-gatherers could find food there. As time went by, people settled along **river** valleys and built harbors so that they could water their crops and trade with their neighbors. In the last few centuries contact between distant peoples and the ability to move raw materials from one place to another in trucks, ships, and planes has begun to change the economic world. Countries that are rich in **natural resources**—oil, gas, metals, and minerals—still have an advantage over those without them. However, even a tiny country such as Singapore, without natural resources of its own, can flourish today. Its strategic location as an Asian port and openness to trade make it an important part of the worldwide **economy.**

Mechanized Farming

Farmers who own vast farms, such as the one above in North America, now use heavy machinery to work the fields efficiently. Tractors that have attachments for plowing, planting, and cultivating get the crops growing. Combine harvesters will cut and process them.

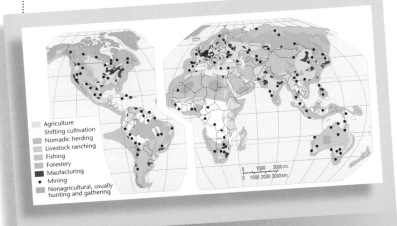

Agriculture
Shifting cultivation
Nomadic herding
Livestock ranching
Fishing
Forestry
Manufacturing
• Mining
Nonagricultural, usually hunting and gathering

0   1000   2000 mi.
0   1000 2000 3000 km.

A World of Products

Economies fall into three main groups: agriculture (including farming, fishing, and forestry), **industry** (such as mining and manufacturing), and the area of private and public services (banking, government, or tourism). The map above shows the major economic activities around the world.

Small Farms

In less developed countries, where farmland is scarce, or where many people share small pieces of land, most farmers till the fields by hand, such as the Chinese women at left planting rice seedlings.

Mining and Refining

Salt miners in Colombia *(left)* remove a thin layer of sand from a vast salt deposit. When they reach the salt, they will dig it up and bag it. This is the simplest form of mining. Other minerals and metals are deposited deep underground, close to **mountain** chains and places where the earth's crust has been folded. Mines produce precious metals such as gold and silver; metals used for industry, including iron, copper, and aluminum; gemstones, such as diamonds and rubies; and coal. Refineries—facilities that purify the raw materials— often operate near the mines.

Industry and Manufacturing

Global Gadget

Refined metals and other materials go to factories that produce machinery or supplies for building anything from houses to watches, footballs, and dentists' drills. Many factories today use the assembly line system. Products roll from one station to another in the factory as workers fasten separate pieces together, paint, polish, and even test the finished items. In some factories, such as the car manufacturer at right, robots do most of the assembly work. Human workers will add to the job at a later stage.

Made by Hand

Not all factory work can be done by machine. Highly skilled workers are needed to craft or assemble parts at this electronics plant in China.

Before you take that first ride around the block with your new bicycle, its parts will already have traveled thousands of miles. Like many everyday objects, a bicycle is made up of parts from several different countries. In one bicycle brand, for example, the frame is made in the United States, the brakes and gears come from Japan, the saddle from Italy, the tires from Germany, the spokes from Switzerland, and the tire rims and hubs from France. The raw materials—the metal and the rubber—come from still other areas of the globe. This one object shows how interconnected the world of economics really is and how much we all depend on others.

Geography and Culture

A culture is a way of life that is shared by a group of people. People in a **culture** speak the same language, eat the same kinds of food, and live in similar houses. A society's culture grows in part from the way people use the resources of their homeland. In Arctic areas, for instance, where there are few plants to eat or use to make clothing, traditional people live on meat-rich diets and fashion clothing from animal skins. The San people of the Kalahari in southern Africa, however, eat more vegetables than meat: roots, nuts, and melons supplemented with meat when hunters can get it. They move around a vast territory because they would soon exhaust plant food sources in any one area. Learning about the **geography** and **climate** of a place can give you many clues about why people live the way they do.

Food

Asian Dinner

The ideal meal for this Chinese-American family is made of numerous dishes of vegetables, rice, and meat. In Asia, food is cooked quickly in small pieces to save fuel. Many Asians use chopsticks, for cooking as well as eating.

Dinner in Europe

In France a family prefers a meal with large portions of a few items, eaten from individual plates with metal forks, knives, and spoons. Many families like to have their biggest meal in the middle of the day.

No Place Like Home

Round Houses

When this African child plays house, he imagines round structures like the ones found in his homeland in Tanzania.

Living Afloat

Tightly packed houseboats in Hong Kong harbor shelter 50,000 people. Some families have lived for generations on these boats, which may also double as places of business for drying fish or for making and selling handicrafts.

Clothing

In France

The faces of children in a French schoolyard show that families from many nations now live in France. The children's clothes—all factory made and similar in style—show that the French live in a manufacturing nation with a cool climate.

Square Houses

Square, angular houses seem normal to this American boy, who made his house out of construction paper.

In Nigeria

Though all share the same heritage and culture, these Nigerian children display a mixture of European and native clothing. No one wears a coat, though; this is a warm climate!

The Global Community

The world is shrinking! Well, not really. But people today can travel to distant lands, meet others from different **cultures,** and do it all very quickly. Knowing about life in other countries is both exciting and troublesome. Many places, such as the teeming city of Dhaka, Bangladesh *(right),* are crowded and poor. Their problems can affect the rest of the world.

Since the end of World War II, people have been on the move in large numbers to leave their countries and seek their fortunes elsewhere. Many more wars and famines, and much more overcrowding and unemployment, have caused people to trek from east to west, from south to north, from rural countries to industrialized ones.

Diseases such as AIDS or influenza can now travel quickly between populations as sick people move between countries. Despite these risks, most people agree that we are all better off for knowing our neighbors.

Asia
3,600 million

Europe
700 million

North America
400 million

Africa
800 million

Australia and Oceania
30 million

South America
300 million

Population Density

The world's population is growing fast: About six billion people will greet the 21st century as better food and medicine increase their life span. Some **continents** are more crowded than others, as the chart above shows, and have different population growth rates. The fastest growing populations live in Africa and **Latin America.**

The Human Race

Marathon runners vie for the lead in a competition designed to foster international friendship as much as national pride. People from every part of the globe are mixing in new ways today. Companies routinely run factories on a number of continents. European countries are introducing an international currency and passport. Adoption agencies place 10,000 overseas babies in U.S. families every year. Worldwide transport systems ensure that immigrants to a new country need not be cut off from their origins. People everywhere are learning to appreciate the rich diversity of humanity's faces.

Migration

Sixty million people go from one country to another each year; many, such as the Vietnamese boat people *(left)* and Rwandan refugees *(below)*, make moves caused by war or hunger. They hope to find new homes elsewhere or to return eventually to their homeland.

The Wired World

Technology is blending cultures every day. Whether their screens display Chinese, as does the computer above, or English, they all use the same kinds of microchips. The Internet connects people, and e-mail sends information, greetings, and jokes from one continent to another in seconds. No matter what its **geography,** no country is isolated from the rest of the world.

Gazetteer Countries of the World A-D

Country	Area sq km	(sq mi.)	Population	Capital
Afghanistan	652,090	(251,773)	24.8 million	Kabul
Albania	28,748	(11,100)	3.3 million	Tirana
Algeria	2,381,741	(919,595)	30.2 million	Algiers
Andorra	453	(175)	0.1 million	Andorra la Vella
Angola	1,246,700	(481,354)	12.0 million	Luanda
Antigua and Barbuda	440	(170)	0.1 million	St. John's
Argentina	2,776,889	(1,068,302)	36.1 million	Buenos Aires
Armenia	30,000	(11,583)	3.8 million	Yerevan
Australia	7,682,300	(2,966,153)	18.7 million	Canberra
Austria	83,856	(32,377)	8.1 million	Vienna
Azerbaijan	87,000	(33,591)	7.7 million	Baku
Bahamas	13,939	(5,382)	0.3 million	Nassau
Bahrain	691	(267)	0.6 million	Manama
Bangladesh	143,998	(55,598)	123.4 million	Dhaka
Barbados	430	(166)	0.3 million	Bridgetown
Belarus	207,600	(80,154)	10.2 million	Minsk
Belgium	30,518	(11,783)	10.2 million	Brussels
Belize	22,965	(8,867)	0.2 million	Belmopan
Benin	112,622	(43,484)	6.0 million	Porto-Novo
Bhutan	47,000	(18,147)	0.8 million	Thimphu
Bolivia	1,098,581	(424,164)	8.0 million	La Paz
Bosnia and Herzegovina	51,129	(19,741)	4.0 million	Sarajevo
Botswana	600,372	(231,805)	1.4 million	Gaborone
Brazil	8,511,347	(3,286,488)	162.1 million	Brasília
Brunei Darussalam	5,765	(2,226)	0.3 million	Bandar Seri Begawan
Bulgaria	110,912	(42,823)	8.3 million	Sofia
Burkina Faso	274,200	(105,869)	11.3 million	Ouagadougou
Burundi	27,834	(10,747)	5.5 million	Bujumbura
Cambodia	181,035	(69,898)	10.8 million	Phnom Penh
Cameroon	475,442	(183,569)	14.3 million	Yaoundé
Canada	9,970,610	(3,849,670)	30.0 million	Ottawa
Cape Verde	4,033	(1,557)	0.4 million	Praia
Central African Republic	622,984	(240,535)	3.4 million	Bangui
Chad	1,284,000	(495,755)	7.4 million	N'Djamena
Chile	756,626	(292,135)	14.8 million	Santiago
China	9,596,961	(3,705,407)	1,249.2 million	Beijing
Colombia	1,138,914	(439,737)	38.6 million	Bogotá
Comoros	1,862	(719)	0.5 million	Moroni
Congo	342,000	(132,047)	2.7 million	Brazzaville
Cook Islands	240	(93)	0.02 million	Rarotonga
Costa Rica	51,100	(19,730)	3.5 million	San José
Côte D'Ivoire	322,463	(124,504)	15.6 million	Yamoussoukro
Croatia	56,538	(21,829)	4.2 million	Zagreb
Cuba	110,861	(42,804)	11.1 million	Havana
Cyprus	5,897	(2,277)	0.7 million	Nicosia
Czech Republic	78,864	(30,450)	10.3 million	Prague
Democratic Republic of Congo	2,345,409	(905,568)	49.0 million	Kinshasa
Denmark	43,092	(16,638)	5.3 million	Copenhagen
Djibouti	23,200	(8,958)	0.7 million	Djibouti
Dominica	751	(290)	0.1 million	Roseau

Official Languages	Continent
Pashtu, Dari	Asia
Albanian, Greek	Europe
Arabic, French	Africa
Catalan, Spanish	Europe
Portuguese, Bantu languages	Africa
English	North America
Spanish	South America
Armenian, Russian	Asia
English	Australia
German	Europe
Azeri, Russian	Asia
English, Creole	North America
Arabic	Asia
Bengali	Asia
English	North America
Belorussian	Europe
Dutch, French, German	Europe
English, Creole, Spanish	North America
French, Fon, African languages	Africa
Dzongkha, Tibetan, Nepali	Asia
Spanish, Aymara, Quechua	South America
Bosnian, Serbian, Croatian	Europe
English, Setswana, African languages	Africa
Portuguese	South America
Malay, English, Chinese	Asia
Bulgarian, Turkish	Europe
French, African languages	Africa
French, Kirundi, Swahili	Africa
Khmer	Asia
French, English, African languages	Africa
English, French	North America
Portuguese, Crioulo	Africa
French, Sango	Africa
French, Arabic, African languages	Africa
Spanish	South America
Chinese	Asia
Spanish	South America
Arabic, French, Comoran	Africa
French, Lingala, Kikongo	Africa
Cook Island Maori	Australia
Spanish	North America
French, African languages	Africa
Croatian, Serbian	Europe
Spanish	North America
Greek, Turkish	Asia
Czech, Polish	Europe
French, African languages	Africa
Danish	Europe
French, Arabic, Somali	Africa
English	North America

Above: Women seek shelter in a dust storm in the Sahara near Djanet, Algeria.

Right: Australia's traffic signs warn of kangaroo crossings.

NEXT
20 km

Left: A girl from Afghanistan sparkles with silver jewelry.

Country	Area sq km	(sq mi.)	Population	Capital
Dominican Republic	48,734	(18,816)	8.3 million	Santo Domingo
Ecuador	283,561	(109,484)	12.2 million	Quito
Egypt	1,001,449	(386,662)	65.5 million	Cairo
El Salvador	21,041	(8,124)	5.8 million	San Salvador
Equatorial Guinea	28,051	(10,831)	0.4 million	Malabo
Eritrea	121,320	(46,842)	3.8 million	Asmara
Estonia	45,100	(17,413)	1.4 million	Tallinn
Ethiopia	1,100,580	(424,934)	58.4 million	Addis Ababa
Fiji	18,274	(7,056)	0.8 million	Suva
Finland	338,145	(130,558)	5.2 million	Helsinki
France	543,965	(210,026)	58.8 million	Paris
French Guiana (French Overseas Department)	90,000	(34,749)	0.2 million	Cayenne
Gabon	267,667	(103,347)	1.2 million	Libreville
Gambia	11,295	(4,361)	1.2 million	Banjul
Georgia	70,000	(27,027)	5.4 million	Tbilisi
Germany	357,046	(137,857)	82.3 million	Berlin
Ghana	238,537	(92,100)	18.9 million	Accra
Greece	131,990	(50,962)	10.5 million	Athens
Greenland (Autonomous part of Denmark)	2,175,600	(840,004)	0.06 million	Godthåb
Grenada	344	(133)	0.1 million	St. George's
Guatemala	108,889	(42,042)	11.6 million	Guatemala City
Guinea	245,857	(94,926)	7.5 million	Conakry
Guinea-Bissau	36,125	(13,948)	1.1 million	Bissau
Guyana	214,969	(83,000)	0.7 million	Georgetown
Haiti	27,750	(10,714)	7.5 million	Port-au-Prince
Honduras	112,088	(43,277)	5.9 million	Tegucigalpa
Hungary	93,030	(35,919)	10.1 million	Budapest
Iceland	103,000	(39,769)	0.3 million	Reykjavik
India	3,287,590	(1,269,346)	988.7 million	New Delhi
Indonesia	1,919,443	(741,101)	207.4 million	Jakarta
Iran	1,648,000	(636,296)	64.1 million	Tehran
Iraq	438,317	(169,235)	21.8 million	Baghdad
Ireland	70,284	(27,137)	3.7 million	Dublin
Israel	20,770	(8,019)	6.0 million	Jerusalem
Italy	301,277	(116,324)	57.7 million	Rome
Jamaica	10,991	(4,244)	2.6 million	Kingston
Japan	377,815	(145,875)	126.4 million	Tokyo
Jordan	91,860	(35,467)	4.6 million	Amman
Kazakhstan	2,717,000	(1,049,039)	15.6 million	Almaty, Astana
Kenya	582,646	(224,961)	28.3 million	Nairobi
Kiribati	717	(277)	0.08 million	Tarawa
Korea, North	120,538	(46,540)	22.2 million	Pyongyang
Korea, South	99,016	(38,230)	46.4 million	Seoul
Kuwait	17,818	(6,880)	1.9 million	Kuwait
Kyrgyzstan	199,000	(76,834)	4.7 million	Bishkek
Laos	236,800	(91,429)	5.3 million	Vientiane
Latvia	64,600	(24,942)	2.4 million	Riga
Lebanon	10,400	(4,015)	4.1 million	Beirut

Official Languages	Continent
Spanish	North America
Spanish, Quechua	South America
Arabic	Africa
Spanish	North America
Spanish, Fang, Bubi	Africa
Afar, Tigrinya, Tigré	Africa
Estonian, Russian	Europe
Amharic, Orominga	Africa
English, Fijian, Hindi	Australia
Finnish, Swedish	Europe
French	Europe
French	South America
French, African languages	Africa
English, Mandinka, Fulani	Africa
Georgian, Russian	Asia
German	Europe
English, Akan, Mossi	Africa
Greek	Europe
Greenlandic, Danish	North America
English	North America
Spanish, Mayan	North America
French, African languages	Africa
Portuguese, Crioulo	Africa
English	South America
French, Creole	North America
Spanish, Creole	North America
Hungarian	Europe
Icelandic	Europe
Hindi, 14 others, English	Asia
Bahasa Indonesian, Javanese	Asia
Persian, Turkish, Kurdish, Arabic	Asia
Arabic, Kurdish	Asia
English, Irish (Gaelic)	Europe
Hebrew, Arabic	Asia
Italian	Europe
English, Creole	North America
Japanese	Asia
Arabic	Asia
Kazakh, Russian	Asia
English, Swahili, African languages	Africa
English, Gilbertese	Australia
Korean	Asia
Korean	Asia
Arabic, English	Asia
Kirghiz, Russian	Asia
Lao	Asia
Latvian, Russian	Europe
Arabic, French	Asia

Children carry flowers attached to palm fronds in a festival in Indonesia.

Gazetteer Countries of the World L-S

Country	Area sq km	(sq mi.)	Population	Capital
Lesotho	30,355	(11,720)	2.1 million	Maseru
Liberia	111,369	(43,000)	2.8 million	Monrovia
Libya	1,759,540	(679,362)	5.7 million	Tripoli
Liechtenstein	160	(62)	0.03 million	Vaduz
Lithuania	65,200	(25,174)	3.7 million	Vilnius
Luxembourg	2,586	(998)	0.4 million	Luxembourg
Macedonia	25,713	(9,928)	2.0 million	Skopje
Madagascar	587,041	(226,658)	14.0 million	Antananarivo
Malawi	118,484	(45,747)	9.8 million	Lilongwe
Malaysia	329,749	(127,317)	22.2 million	Kuala Lumpur
Maldives	298	(115)	0.3 million	Male
Mali	1,240,192	(478,841)	10.1 million	Bamako
Malta	316	(122)	0.4 million	Valletta
Marshall Islands	181	(70)	0.1 million	Majuro
Mauritania	1,030,700	(397,955)	2.5 million	Nouakchott
Mauritius	2,040	(788)	1.2 million	Port Louis
Mexico	1,958,201	(756,066)	97.5 million	Mexico City
Micronesia	702	(271)	0.1 million	Palikir
Moldova	43,000	(13,127)	4.2 million	Chisinau
Monaco	1.9	(0.6)	0.03 million	Monaco
Mongolia	1,565,000	(604,250)	2.4 million	Ulan Bator
Morocco	712,550	(275,117)	27.7 million	Rabat
Mozambique	799,380	(308,642)	18.6 million	Maputo
Myanmar	676,552	(261,218)	47.1 million	Yangon
Namibia	824,292	(318,261)	1.6 million	Windhoek
Nauru	21	(8)	0.01 million	Yaren
Nepal	140,797	(54,362)	23.7 million	Kathmandu
Netherlands	41,500	(16,023)	15.7 million	Amsterdam
New Zealand	269,057	(103,883)	3.8 million	Wellington
Nicaragua	130,000	(50,193)	4.8 million	Managua
Niger	1,267,000	(489,191)	10.1 million	Niamey
Nigeria	923,768	(365,669)	121.8 million	Abuja
Norway	324,220	(125,182)	4.4 million	Oslo
Oman	212,457	(82,030)	2.5 million	Muscat
Pakistan	796,095	(307,374)	141.9 million	Islamabad
Palau, Republic of	487	(188)	0.02 million	Koror
Panama	77,082	(29,762)	2.8 million	Panama City
Papua New Guinea	461,691	(178,260)	4.3 million	Port Moresby
Paraguay	406,752	(157,048)	5.2 million	Asunción
Peru	1,285,220	(496,225)	26.1 million	Lima
Philippines	300,000	(115,831)	75.3 million	Manila
Poland	312,677	(120,725)	38.7 million	Warsaw
Portugal	92,389	(35,672)	10.0 million	Lisbon
Qatar	11,000	(4,247)	0.5 million	Doha
Romania	237,500	(91,699)	22.5 million	Bucharest
Russia	17,075,000	(6,592,692)	146.9 million	Moscow
Rwanda	26,338	(10,169)	8.0 million	Kigali
St. Kitts and Nevis	261	(101)	0.04 million	Basseterre
St. Lucia	617	(238)	0.1 million	Castries
St. Vincent and the Grenadines	388	(150)	0.1 million	Kingstown

Official Languages	Continent
Sesotho	Africa
English, African languages	Africa
Arabic, English, Italian	Africa
German	Europe
Lithuanian, Russian, Polish	Europe
Letzeburgesch, French, German	Europe
Macedonian, Croatian, Serbian	Europe
French, Malagasy	Africa
Chichewa, English, African languages	Africa
Malay, many others	Asia
Divehi	Asia
French	Africa
Maltese, English	Europe
English, Marshall, Japanese	Australia
Arabic, French	Africa
English, Creole, Bhojpuri	Africa
Spanish, Indian languages	North America
English, Trukese, Ponapean	Australia
Romanian, Moldovan, Russian	Europe
French, Monegasque, Italian	Europe
Khalkha Mongolian	Asia
Arabic, Berber, French	Africa
Portuguese, African languages	Africa
Myanmar (Burmese), Karen, Shan	Asia
Afrikaans, English, German	Africa
Nauruan, English	Australia
Nepali	Asia
Dutch	Europe
English, Maori	Australia
Spanish	North America
French, Hausa, Djerma	Africa
English, Hausa, Ibo	Africa
Norwegian	Europe
Arabic	Asia
Urdu, Punjabi, Sindhi	Asia
Palauan, English	Australia
Spanish, English	North America
English, indigenous languages	Australia
Spanish, Guaraní	South America
Spanish, Quechua, Aymara	South America
Filipino, English	Asia
Polish	Europe
Portuguese	Europe
Arabic	Asia
Romanian, Hungarian, German	Europe
Russian	Europe
French, Kinyarwanda, Swahili	Africa
English	North America
English	North America
English	North America

Bananas take center stage at this market stall in Mexico.

Left: A rainbow frames wooden houses in Norway.

Below: A performer in Morocco entertains with snake tricks.

Gazetteer Countries of the World S-Z

Country	Area sq km	(sq mi.)	Population	Capital
San Marino	61	(24)	0.03 million	San Marino
São Tomé and Príncipe	964	(372)	0.2 million	São Tomé
Saudi Arabia	2,149,690	(830,000)	20.2 million	Riyadh
Senegal	196,722	(75,955)	9.0 million	Dakar
Seychelles	453	(175)	0.1 million	Victoria
Sierra Leone	71,740	(27,699)	4.6 million	Freetown
Singapore	618	(239)	3.9 million	Singapore
Slovakia	49,006	(18,921)	5.4 million	Bratislava
Slovenia	20,251	(7,719)	2.0 million	Ljubljana
Solomon Islands	28,450	(10,985)	0.4 million	Honiara
Somalia	637,657	(246,201)	10.7 million	Mogadishu
South Africa	1,221,037	(471,445)	38.9 million	Pretoria, Cape Town, Bloemfontein
Spain	504,782	(194,897)	39.4 million	Madrid
Sri Lanka	65,610	(25,332)	18.9 million	Colombo
Sudan	2,505,813	(967,500)	28.5 million	Khartoum
Suriname	163,265	(63,037)	0.4 million	Paramaribo
Swaziland	17,364	(6,704)	1.0 million	Mbabane
Sweden	449,964	(173,732)	8.9 million	Stockholm
Switzerland	41,288	(15,941)	7.1 million	Bern
Syria	184,004	(71,044)	15.6 million	Damascus
Taiwan	36,000	(13,900)	21.7 million	Taipei
Tajikistan	143,000	(55,213)	6.1 million	Dushanbe
Tanzania	945,087	(364,900)	30.6 million	Dar es Salaam
Thailand	514,000	(198,457)	61.1 million	Bangkok
Togo	56,785	(21,925)	4.9 million	Lomé
Tonga	699	(270)	0.11 million	Nukualofa
Trinidad and Tobago	5,130	(1,981)	1.3 million	Port of Spain
Tunisia	163,610	(63,170)	9.5 million	Tunis
Turkey	779,452	(300,948)	64.8 million	Ankara
Turkmenistan	488,000	(188,418)	4.7 million	Ashgabat
Tuvalu	26	(10)	0.01 million	Funafuti
Uganda	236,036	(91,134)	21.0 million	Kampala
Ukraine	604,000	(233,206)	50.3 million	Kiev
United Arab Emirates	83,600	(32,278)	2.7 million	Abu Dhabi
United Kingdom	244,100	(94,248)	59.1 million	London
United States	9,372,614	(3,618,770)	270.2 million	Washington, D.C.
Uruguay	176,215	(68,037)	3.2 million	Montevideo
Uzbekistan	447,000	(172,588)	24.1 million	Tashkent
Vanuatu	14,760	(5,700)	0.2 million	Port-Vila
Vatican City	0.4	(0.2)	0.0008 million	————
Venezuela	912,050	(352,144)	23.3 million	Caracas
Vietnam	329,556	(127,242)	78.5 million	Hanoi
Western Samoa	2,831	(1,093)	0.2 million	Apia
Yemen	527,968	(203,850)	15.8 million	Sanaa
Yugoslavia	102,173	(39,450)	10.6 million	Belgrade
Zambia	752,614	(290,586)	9.5 million	Lusaka
Zimbabwe	390,580	(150,804)	11.0 million	Harare

Official Languages	Continent
Italian	Europe
Portuguese	Africa
Arabic	Asia
French, African languages	Africa
English, French, Creole	Africa
English, Krio, Mende	Africa
English, Malay, Chinese	Asia
Slovak, Hungarian	Europe
Slovenian, Croatian, Serbian	Europe
English, Melanesian languages	Australia
Somali, Arabic, English	Africa
Afrikaans, English, Bantu languages	Africa
Spanish, Catalan, Galician	Europe
Sinhalese, Tamil, English	Asia
Arabic, English, African languages	Africa
Dutch, Sranan, Tongo	South America
English, siSwati	Africa
Swedish	Europe
German, French, Italian	Europe
Arabic, Kurdish	Asia
Chinese	Asia
Tajik, Russian	Asia
Swahili, English, African languages	Africa
Thai	Asia
French, Kabye, Ewe	Africa
Tongan, English	Australia
English, Creole	North America
Arabic, French	Africa
Turkish, Kurdish, Arabic	Asia
Turkmen, Russian	Asia
Tuvaluan, English	Australia
English, Swahili, Luganda	Africa
Ukrainian, Russian	Europe
Arabic	Asia
English, Welsh, Gaelic	Europe
English	North America
Spanish	South America
Uzbek, Russian	Asia
Bislama, English, French	Australia
Italian, Latin	Europe
Spanish	South America
Vietnamese	Asia
Samoan, English	Australia
Arabic	Asia
Serbian, Hungarian, Albanian, Croatian	Europe
English, Bantu languages	Africa
English, Shona, Ndebele	Africa

In Sri Lanka many young men spend their days perched on poles to fish.

Gilded figures of dancers support the walls of a temple in Thailand.

Wind-eroded rocks give Arches National Park in Utah, U.S.A., its name.

Picture Credits

—map by John Drummond—CORBIS/Michael S. Yamashita; CORBIS/Tom Bean. **59:** Bodleian Library, Oxford, England (Ms.Douce 383 folio 12v) (inset); Adam Woolfitt/Robert Harding Picture Library, London; CORBIS/Bettmann—© Doug Corrance/Still Moving Picture Company, Edinburgh, Scotland; Robert Kenneth Wilson/Mary Evans Picture Library, London (inset); © John Miller/Robert Harding Picture Library, London. **60, 61:** Map by John Drummond; © Picture Finders/Bavaria Bildagentur, Munich, Germany; +49/Visum/Wolfgang Korall, Hamburg, Germany—CORBIS/Steve Raymer—CORBIS/Bob Krist; © Mats Wibe Lund-EGILL SIGURDSSON, Icelandic Photo, Reykjavik, Iceland; CORBIS/Macduff Everton; CORBIS/Ludovic Maisant. **62:** Map by John Drummond; CORBIS/Owen Franken—© P. Van Riel/Explorer/Photo Researchers; CORBIS/Dave G. Houser. **63:** CORBIS/Wolfgang Kaehler; Waltraud Klammet, Ohlstadt—Laenderpress, Mainz, Germany; Visum/Thomas Pflaum, Hamburg, Germany; art by Maria DiLeo. **64, 65:** Map by John Drummond; Bernard Wolf/National Geographic; CORBIS/Jerry Cooke—Claudio Corrivetti, Rome—CORBIS/Galen Rowell; © F. Le Diascorn/Rapho; © Tony Stone Images; Mike Newton/Robert Harding Picture Library, London. **66, 67:** Map by John Drummond; James Stanfield/National Geographic Society; Visum/Thomas Pflaum, Hamburg, Germany; CORBIS/Adam Woolfitt—CORBIS/Peter Wilson; Schapowalow/Nebe, Hamburg, Germany; CORBIS/Robert Dowling; CORBIS/Roger Wood; AIPS/National Geographic Society Image Collection. **68, 69:** Map by John Drummond; © N. Rakhmanov/Agence ANA, Paris; CORBIS/Dean Conger—AP/Wide World Photos; © Jeff Greenberg; Laenderpress, Mainz, Germany; Horst von Irmer, Internationales Bildarchiv, Munich, Germany. **70:** Dale Brown—map by John Drummond. **71:** © 1995 WorldSat International and J. Knighton/Photo Researchers. **72:** Map by John Drummond; Dean Conger/National Geographic Society; CORBIS/Dean Conger—Dean Conger/National Geographic Society; © Frans Lanting/Minden Pictures; © Tom Ang/NHPA, Ardingly, Sussex, England; art by John Drummond (inset); Tor Eigeland/Aramco World. **74, 75:** Map by John Drummond; Fritz Dressler, Worpswede; CORBIS/Dean Conger (inset); Nik Wheeler/Aramco World—© Jim Brandenburg/Minden Pictures; Robert Harding Picture Library, London; Bildarchiv W. Klammet/J. Beck, Ohlstadt. **76, 77:** Art by John Drummond; © Louis Audoubert/Scope; CORBIS/Sheldon Collins—Anthony Verlag/Dr. Reisel, Beuerberg, Germany; © 1994 Peter Menzel/Material World. **78:** Map by John Drummond; © 1983 Steve McCurry/Magnum—James Burke; © James Strachan/Robert Harding Picture Library, London. **79:** Roland and Sabrina Michaud—CORBIS/Johnathan Blair; James P. Blair/National Geographic Society. **80:** © Stephanie Maze—map by John Drummond—CORBIS/Charles and Josette Lenars; CORBIS/Michael S. Yamashita. **81:** CORBIS/Michael Freeman—CORBIS/Gary Braasch; CORBIS. **82:** Map by John Drummond; © Amos Schliack, Hamburg, Germany; © Michael Freeman, London—Steve McCurry/National Geographic Society; © Michael S. Yamashita/Woodfin Camp (2); Dale Brown. **84:** Pascal and Maria Maréchaux—map by John Drummond—CORBIS/Marc Granger; Dale Brown. **85:** James Stanfield/National Geographic Society; © SuperStock (inset)

—SuperStock; © Robert Azzi/Woodfin Camp. **86:** Art Wolfe/Art Wolfe, Inc.—map by John Drummond. **87:** © Tom Van Sant/Stock Market. **88, 89:** Map by John Drummond; AP/Wide World Photos/Bruno Fablet/Presse Sports; Dale Brown—Adam Woolfitt/Robert Harding Picture Library, London; CORBIS/Roger Wood; CORBIS/Caroline Penn. **90, 91:** Map by John Drummond; Co Rentmeester; © 1993 Peter Menzel/Material World—art by Maria DiLeo; Chuck Fishman/PNI; CORBIS/Wolfgang Kaehler; from *A Is for Africa* by Ifeoma Onyefulu, published by Frances Lincoln Ltd., copyright 1993, reproduced by permission of Frances Lincoln Ltd., 4 Torriano Mews, Torriano Ave., London NW5 2RZ. **92:** Paul Q. Fuqua—map by John Drummond—Dale Brown—Kenneth Garret/National Geographic Society; Adrian Warren/Ardea Limited, London. **93:** © Steve Turner, Oxford Scientific Films, Long Hanborough, Oxfordshire, England—Emory Kristof/National Geographic Society; map by John Drummond (inset); CORBIS/Michael and Patricia Fogden. **94, 95:** Map by John Drummond—Robert Caputo/PNI; James Sugar/PNI; © Dr. Georg Gerster—George F. Mobley/National Geographic Society; © K. & K. Ammann/Bruce Coleman, Inc. **96:** Visum/Manfred Schamberg, Hamburg, Germany—map by John Drummond—CORBIS/Wolfgang Kaehler; © Anthony Bannister/NHPA, Ardingly, Sussex, England. **97:** Anthony Verlag, Beuerberg, Germany; CORBIS/Peter Turnley—The Hutchison Library, London (2). **98:** © 1995 Paul Steel/Stock Market—map by John Drummond. **99:** © Tom Van Sant/Stock Market. **100, 101:** © Wayne Lawler/Photo Researchers; © Reg Morrison/AUSCAPE; Jean-Paul Ferrero/Ardea Limited, London (inset); CORBIS/Paul A. Souders—© A.N.T/NHPA, Ardingly, Sussex, England—© Jean-Paul Ferrero/Ardea Limited, London; E. R. Degginger/Color-Pic, Inc. **102:** © Michael McIntyre/The Hutchison Library, London; David Hiser/National Geographic Society. **103:** CORBIS/Wolfgang Kaehler; CORBIS/Jack Fields—Bruno Barbier/© Tony Stone Images; CORBIS/Jack Fields. **104:** U.S. Geological Survey/Science Photo Library/Science Source/Photo Researchers—globe by John Drummond; Mary Evans Picture Library, London; map by John Drummond. **105:** C. J. Gilbert, British Antarctic Survey, Cambridge; Ben Osborne/Oxford Scientific Films, Long Hanborough, Oxfordshire, England (inset)—© 1990, Amon Carter Museum, Fort Worth, Tex., bequest of Eliot Porter; Mike Pattisall; CORBIS/Kit Kittle. **106:** Geosystems; © 1996 Bill Stormont/Stock Market—© Grabinger/Laenderpress, Mainz, Germany. **107:** CORBIS/Jeremy Horner; CORBIS/Karl Weatherly—© 1990 Jon Feingersh/Stock Market—CORBIS/Kevin R. Morris. **108, 109:** Nick Gordon/Ardea Limited, London; G. Bosio/Hoa Qui, Paris—© SuperStock—Michel Viard/Jacana, Paris; © 1986 Frans Lanting/Minden Pictures—Monique Burgerhoff Molder; Robert Moss Photography, Alexandria, Va.—X. Richer; © Paul Dowd/Eye Ubiquitous, Shoreham, West Sussex, England. **110:** Map by John Drummond; Karen Kasmauski. **111:** Manuela Machado/AllSport—Rex USA; © Wesley Bocxe/Photo Researchers; CORBIS/Keren Su. **113:** CORBIS/Bernard and Catherine Desjeux—CORBIS/Australian Picture Library—CORBIS/Ric Ergenbright. **115:** CORBIS/Lindsay Hebberd. **117:** Paul Q. Fuqua—Dale Brown (2). **119:** CORBIS/Jeremy Horner—Dale Brown—Paul Q. Fuqua.

Glossary of Terms

Acid rain (**a**–sihd rayn) Rainwater that contains concentrations of acid-forming chemicals.

Alpine (**al**–pyne) Relating to high elevations, usually above the tree line, where trees cannot grow.

Altiplano (ahl–**ti**–pluh–noh) A high plain or plateau between higher mountains.

Altitude Height above sea level.

Aquifer (**ah**–kwuh–fuhr) An underground reservoir of water in a layer of porous rock.

Archipelago (ar–kuh–**pel**–uh–goh) A group or chain of islands in a large body of water.

Arctic Circle (**ark**–tik **sur**–kuhl) An imaginary circle parallel to and 66½° north of the equator. The area inside the circle is referred to as the Arctic. A similar circle defines the Antarctic.

Atoll (**a**–tohl) A ring-shaped coral island, surrounding a shallow body of water.

Autonomous (ah–**tahn**–uh–muhss) Having self-government as a right, without control from an outside government.

Biome (**bye**–ohm) One of the major types of plant and animal communities determined by its climate and geography. Earth has 10 major biomes: savanna, grassland, desert, chaparral, tropical rain forest, temperate rain forest, deciduous forest, coniferous forest, tundra, and polar region.

Cartography (noun, **cartographer**) (kar–**tah**–gruh–fee, kar–**tah**–gruh–fer) The art of making maps.

Climate (**klye**–muht) The weather patterns of a region over a long period of time.

Compass rose (**kuhm**–puhss **rohs**) A design on a map that indicates direction, especially north.

Conifer (adjective, **coniferous**) (**kon**–uh–fuhr, kon–**if**–fuhr-us) An evergreen tree or shrub, with needlelike leaves that form cones.

Continent (**kon**-tuh-nent) A large landmass that rises above the ocean floor; one of the seven major landmasses: Africa, Europe, Asia, Australia, Antarctica, North America, and South America.

Cultivar (**kuhl**–tuh–var) A plant produced by selective breeding.

Culture (**kuhl**–chuhr) The way of life of a group of people that is passed on, including language, beliefs, customs, and arts.

Debris (duh–**bree**) Fragments of rock, pebbles, and sand.

Deciduous (duh–**sihd**–yoo–uhss) Having leaves that turn colors and are shed every fall.

Delta (**del**–tuh) Lowland at the mouth of a river, shaped by silt and sand deposits.

Dependency (duh–**pen**–duhn–see) A separate territory under the authority of a different country.

Desert (**de**–surt) A land area that on average receives 250 mm (10 in.) or less of precipitation a year.

Economy (i–**kon**–uh–mee) The production, distribution, and consumption of goods and services in a country.

Ecosystem (**ee**–koh–siss–tuhm) The interactions among living and nonliving things in an area, such as soil, water, climate, plants, and animals.

Environment (en–**vye**–ruhn–muhnt) The climate, soil, and living things with which an organism interacts and which determine its form and survival.

Equator (ee–**kway**–tuhr) An imaginary line around earth's middle, halfway between the North and South Poles; 0° of latitude.

Erosion (verb, **erode**) (i–**roh**–shuhn, i–**rode**) The breaking down of rock or soil by water, ice, or temperature changes and the movement of the particles by water, ice, wind, or gravity.

Ethnic (**eth**–nik) Having to do with a group of people united by their culture.

Fjord (**fyord**) A long, narrow ocean inlet with steep sides that extends far inland.

Forest (**for**–ist) A large area covered with trees and underbrush.

Geographer (gee–**ah**–gruh–fuhr) A person who studies and explains geography.

Geography (adjective, **geographic**) (gee–**ah**–gruh–fee, gee–ah–**graf**–ic) The study of the earth's surface and the relationship between people and their environment, the distribution of plants, animals, and people, and the features of land, ocean, and climate.

Geyser (**gye**–suhr) Underground hot spring that periodically shoots steam and hot water into the air.

Grassland (**gras**–land) Land covered with grasses, where yearly precipitation averages between 250 and 750 mm (10 and 30 in.).

Ground water (**grownd** wa–tuhr) Water beneath the earth's surface that supplies springs and wells.

Gyre (**jire**) A circular movement of the ocean currents, turning clockwise in the Northern Hemisphere, counterclockwise in the Southern Hemisphere.

Habitat (**hab**–i–tat) The natural environment in which a plant or an animal lives.

Hill (**hil**) Land that rises above the surrounding area, usually with an elevation of less than 300 m (1,000 ft.). One of four major landforms along with plains, plateaus, and mountains.

Ice Age (**eyess** aje) One of several periods in earth's history during which much of the planet's surface was covered with ice. The last Ice Age ended about 10,000 years ago.

Indigenous (in–**dih**–juh–nuhss) Belonging to a place by birth.

Industry (**in**–duh–stree) An activity that produces a product by extracting natural resources, such as mining, or by processing and manufacturing goods.

Island (**eye**–luhnd) A body of land, smaller than a continent, surrounded by water.

Isthmus (**iss**–muhss) A narrow strip of land with water on two sides, connecting two larger areas of land.

Latin America (la–tuhn uh–mayr–i–kuh) Mexico and Central and South America.

Latitude (la–ti–tood) The distance north or south of the equator expressed in degrees. Degrees of latitude begin at 0° at the equator and are measured northward to 90° of north latitude at the North Pole, and southward to 90° of south latitude at the South Pole.

Lichen (lye–khuhn) Plants that are made up of an alga and a fungus and that grow on rocks or trees.

Loess (loh–uhss) A deposit of particles of windblown silt or dust.

Longitude (lon–juh–tood) The distance, expressed in degrees, east or west of an imaginary line called the prime meridian, which runs from the North Pole through Greenwich, England, to the South Pole. Lines of longitude go from 0° to 180° east and west of the prime meridian.

Map projection (map pruh–jek–shuhn) The transferring of features from the curved surface of the earth onto a flat surface. A Mercator projection casts a map of the earth onto a cylinder that distorts areas at the poles.

Monsoon (mon–soon) A seasonal wind that is found especially in Asia. A monsoon produces dry and wet seasons.

Mountain (mown–tuhn) Land that rises 300 m (1,000 ft.) or more; one of four major landforms along with plains, plateaus, and hills.

Mouth (mowth) The place where a stream or river ends by flowing into a lake or an ocean.

Natural resource (nat–chur–uhl ree–sorss) Anything that can be consumed or used by people that is provided by the natural environment, such as trees, minerals, gemstones, and petroleum.

Nocturnal (nok–tur–nuhl) Active at night.

Nomads (adjective, nomadic) (noh–mads, noh–mad-ic) People, usually herders, who wander from place to place in search of food and water for their animals, usually seasonally and in a well-defined area.

Ocean (oh–shuhn) The large bodies of salt water that cover two-thirds of the earth's surface.

Organic Chemical compounds that are found only in plants and animals.

Pampas (pom–puhs) Extensive grasslands of South America.

Peninsula (puh–nihn–suh–lah) A body of land jutting out into water from a larger landmass.

Permafrost (puhr–muh–frost) A permanently frozen layer below the earth's surface.

Photosynthesis (foh–toh–sin–thuh–siss) The process in which chlorophyll-bearing plants use water, carbon dioxide, and sunlight to produce sugars and starches.

Physical (fis–uh–kuhl) The exterior features of the earth.

Plain (playn) A vast expanse of generally flat land; one of the four major landforms along with plateaus, hills, and mountains.

Plateau (pla–toh) A large, level area rising above the surrounding region on at least one side.

Plate tectonics (playt tek–ton–iks) The theory that the earth's crust is made up of plates that are constantly moving.

Prairie (prayr–ee) Temperate grasslands of North America.

Precipitation (pri–sip–i–tay–shuhn) The forms of water that fall to the ground from the atmosphere: mist, rain, sleet, hail, or snow.

Rain forest (rayn for–ist) A dense forest of broad-leaved evergreens, vines, and sparse undergrowth that receives an average of 2,000 mm (80 in.) of rain a year.

River (riv–uhr) A large natural stream of water that flows into another river, lake, or ocean.

Sanskrit (san–skrit) A language of ancient India and Hinduism.

Savanna (suh–van–uh) Tropical grassland with scattered trees, where a long, dry period alternates with a short, wet season.

Scale (skayl) A line on a map that is used to represent the relationship between the distance that is measured on the map and the actual distance on the ground.

Silt (sihlt) Particles of soil or sand that are moved and deposited by water, ice, or wind.

Staple (stay–puhl) The chief product of an area; coffee is a staple of Colombia. Also a product used regularly; rice is a staple crop in many countries.

Steppe Dry, temperate grasslands of southeastern Europe and Asia.

Strait (strayt) A narrow passage of water connecting two larger bodies of water.

Temperate (tem–puh–ruht) An area of mild climate.

Terrain (tuh–rayn) An area of land, or the physical features on an area of land.

Tree line Upper limit to forest growth on mountains, where wind and weather are too severe for trees to grow; timberline.

Tributary (trib–yuh–tayr–ee) A stream that empties into a larger river.

Tundra (tuhn–druh) A treeless plain with low vegetation that is found mainly in Arctic and sub-Arctic areas with permanently frozen subsoil.

Water cycle (waw–tur sye–kuhl) The movement of water between the atmosphere, oceans, and the earth through evaporation, condensation, and precipitation; the hydrological cycle.

Weather (weth–ur) The state of the atmosphere in terms of clouds, temperature, humidity, pressure, precipitation, and wind.

Yurt A circular tent made of felt or animal skins used by nomads in Asia.

Index

Index

Time-Life Education, Inc. is a division of Time Life Inc.

TIME LIFE INC.

PRESIDENT and CEO: George Artandi
CHIEF OPERATING OFFICER: Mary Davis Holt

TIME-LIFE EDUCATION, INC.
PRESIDENT: Mary Davis Holt
MANAGING EDITOR: Mary J. Wright

Time-Life Student Library
SERIES EDITOR: Jean Burke Crawford

WORLD GEOGRAPHY
EDITOR: Karin Kinney
Associate Editor/Research and Writing: Lisa Krause
Series Picture Associate: Lisa Groseclose
Editorial Assistant: Maria Washington
Picture Coordinator: Daryl Beard

Designed by: Maria DiLeo, 3r1 Group

Special Contributors: Janet Cave, Patricia Daniels, Mark Galan, Jocelyn Lindsay, Donna Lucey, Jim Lynch, Susan Perry (text); Patti Cass, (research), Barbara Klein (index).
Senior Copyeditor: Judith Klein
Correspondents: Maria Vincenza Aloisi (Paris), Christine Hinze (London), Elisabeth Kraemer-Singh (Bonn), Angelika Lemmer (Bonn), Christina Lieberman (New York).
Editorial Interns: Renesa Bell, Lenese Stephens, Tonya Wilson.

Vice President of Marketing and Publisher: Rosalyn McPherson Andrews
Vice President of Sales: Robert F. Sheridan
Director of Book Production: Patricia Pascale
Director of Publishing Technology: Betsi McGrath
Director of Photography and Research: John Conrad Weiser
Marketing Manager: Michele Stegmaier
Production Manager: Carolyn Clark
Quality Assurance Manager: James King
Chief Librarian: Louise D. Forstall
Direct Marketing Consultant: Barbara Erlandson

Consultants:

Tim Beach, Ph.D., is assistant professor of geography and environmental science in Georgetown University's program in Science, Technology, and International Affairs in the School of Foreign Service. His research investigates the relationships between the soils-geomorphic environment and people in the Corn Belt of the United States, the Yucatán of Mexico, Belize, Guatemala, Syria, and Turkey. He teaches courses on the environmental sciences (climatology, hydrology, geomorphology, and environmental management) and how these relate to environmental management and policy.

Gil Crippen has been teaching geography in the Newport News Public School Division in Virginia for 33 years. He is currently teaching three levels of geography in the International Baccalaureate Program at Warwick High School and is the coordinator of the German-Norwegian Student-to-Student Exchange Program between Newport News and Sotra, Norway, and Altenkirchen, Germany. He is the recipient of numerous awards, including the Virginia Social Studies Educator of the Year, and has written curriculum guides for ninth-grade world geography.

First printing. Printed in U.S.A.
School and library distribution by Time-Life Education, P.O. Box 85026, Richmond, Virginia 23285-5026.
Telephone: 1-800-449-2010
Internet: WWW.TIMELIFEEDU.COM

TIME-LIFE is a trademark of Time Warner Inc. U.S.A.

Library of Congress Cataloging-in-Publication Data
World geography.
    p. cm. — (Time-Life student library)
    Includes index.
    Summary: Examines mapmaking, the Earth's surface and habitats, and the global community, as well as focusing on the economy, culture, and people of the individual continents.
    ISBN 0-7835-1355-0
    1. Geography—Juvenile literature. [1. Geography.]
I. Time-Life Books. II. Series.
G133.W85   1999
910—dc21   99-13762
                                                                      CIP
                                                                       AC

OTHER PUBLICATIONS

TIME-LIFE KIDS
Library of First Questions and
    Answers
A Child's First Library of Learning
I Love Math
Nature Company Discoveries
Understanding Science & Nature

HISTORY
Our American Century
World War II
What Life Was Like
The American Story
Voices of the Civil War
The American Indians
Lost Civilizations
Mysteries of the Unknown
Time Frame
The Civil War
Cultural Atlas

SCIENCE/NATURE
Voyage Through the Universe

DO IT YOURSELF
Total Golf
How to Fix It
The Time-Life Complete Gardener
Home Repair and Improvement
The Art of Woodworking

COOKING
Weight Watchers® Smart Choice
    Recipe Collection
Great Taste–Low Fat
Williams-Sonoma Kitchen Library

For information on and a full description of any of the Time-Life Books series listed above, please call 1-800-621-7026 or write:

Reader Information
Time-Life Customer Service
P.O. Box C-32068
Richmond, Virginia 23261-2068